On The Anzac Trail

On The Anzac Trail

The Experiences of a New Zealand Soldier
in Egypt and Gallipoli During the Great War

"Anzac"

LEONAUR

On The Anzac Trail
The Experiences of a New Zealand Soldier
in Egypt and Gallipoli During the Great War
by "Anzac"

First published under the title
On The Anzac Trail

Leonaur is an imprint
of Oakpast Ltd

ISBN: 978-0-85706-264-2(hardcover)
ISBN: 978-0-85706-263-5 (softcover)

http://www.leonaur.com

Contents

TO THE MEN

By Way of Advertisement

This is the story of the Anzacs. It is told by one of the New Zealanders who was with them in Egypt, was present at the landing, and who did his little best to uphold the honour of Maoriland in the long and grim Battle of the Trenches. It is the tale of a man in the ranks. It is told without gloss or varnish. *And it is true.*

Komate! Komate!
Kaora! Kaora!
Komate! Komate!
Kaora! Kaora!
Tene Te Tonga Te,
Pohuru Uru;
Nana È Tiki Mai,
Whaka Whiti Tera—
Hupani! Hupani! Hupani!
Kupani È Whiti Tera!

Which is also true.

CHAPTER 1

Joining Up

When the Great War struck Europe I was living with my people in Ireland. I had served in the South African campaign, so, of course, I realised that it was up to me to roll up again and do my bit towards keeping the old rag flying. It's a queer thing, but let a man once go on the war-path and it's all the odds to a strap ring he's off again, full cry, to the sound of the bugle. I reckon it's in the Britisher's blood; he kind of imbibes it along with his mother's milk. When all's said and done we are a fighting breed. A sporting crowd, too, and we tackle war much as we would a game of football—or a big round-up in the Never-Never.

When England took off the gloves to Germany I knew the Colonies wouldn't hang back long. They breed men on the fringes of our Empire. Hence I wasn't surprised when I saw a notice in the papers calling on all New Zealanders, or men who had seen service with the Maorilanders in South Africa, to roll up at the High Commissioner's office in London, to be trained for service with the "Down Under" contingents. Well, I had lived for years in New Zealand, and had fought Boers time and again side by side with New Zealand troops, so I sent in my name right away. In due course I received a polite letter of thanks, and was told to turn up at the office on a certain date, to be examined and attested. I did so, and in company with some two hundred other Colonials was put through the eyesight, hearing, and other tests, said "ninety-nine" to the doctor's satisfaction, and was duly passed as fit for service.

And now began a period of stress and strenuous life. Morning after morning we repaired to Wandsworth Common, there to acquaint ourselves with the intricacies of "Right turn," "Left turn," "Form fours," etc., under the tutelage of certain drill-sergeants of leathern lungs and bibulous-looking noses. At noon we knocked off for an hour and a half, repairing for refreshment to a house of entertainment which stood fairly "adjacent" to our drill ground. Here we very soon found that our instructors' looks did not belie them. However, we consoled ourselves with the reflection that English beer was cheap as drinks went, and that all things come to an end in this world. The afternoons were repetitions of the mornings, with the added attraction of a largish audience composed principally of nursemaids and infants in arms—and prams. The audience enjoyed our efforts if we, the actors, didn't. It was thirsty work.

During this period we lived in London, "finding" ourselves, but receiving a slight increase of pay in lieu of quarters and rations. It's a gay city is the Rio London. Our pockets suffered, hence most of us, although we growled on principle (being Colonials), were secretly relieved in mind when the order came to transfer to Salisbury Plain, there to camp in tents until such time as huts should be prepared for us.

I think we all enjoyed our stay on the "Plain"—a sad misnomer, by the way, as I never ran across a hillier plain in my life. It was autumn in England, and when we first arrived, except for cold nights the weather was really good—for England! It soon broke, however, and we sampled to the full the joys of sleeping on rain-soaked blankets and ploughing our way through the sticky chalk soil that hereabouts is so strongly in evidence. Hence we weren't sorry to transfer our swags to the more kindly shelter of the huts. In fact, we took possession of them before they were quite ready for occupancy, electing to complete the work ourselves. Most of us were "bush carpenters," so the job was right into our hands.

Our camp lay within two miles of Bulford village, a kind of Sleepy Hollow inhabited by a bovine-looking breed, whose mouths seemed intended for beer-drinking but not talking which, in a way, was just as well, for when they did make a remark it was all Greek to us. We wakened the place up a bit, however, and the Canadians, who settled down to the tune of over five thousand round about us, nobly seconded our efforts, so I reckon the power of speech was restored to the villagers—after we left! For all I know they may be talking yet. Come to think it over in cold blood, they had cause to.

Those Kanucks were a hefty lot, and blessed with real top-knotch powers of absorption. They were sports, too. We beat them at Rugby football, but they took their change back at soccer. Honours were even, I think, at drill, but they drank our canteen dry every night. You see, there were five thousand of them and only a little over two hundred of us. As they were inclined to talk a bit in their cups we were forced to mount an armed guard in the canteen. The guard's principal duty was to stop scrapping on the premises, and the first sign of "peeling" operations being indulged in was the signal to round up the mob. Once outside, however, they could do as they liked. And they generally did! Discoloured optics and flattened nasal appendages soon ceased to be objects of curiosity down our location. On the whole we got on well with them, and we had many things in common. Poor fellows, they got stuck into it cruelly in France, between German gas and overpowering numbers, but they showed real grit right through—just as we who had been camp-mates with them knew they would.

Barring the heavy frosts, the rain, and the foot-deep mud, things weren't so bad in camp. The tucker was really good and there was plenty of it; the huts were, on the whole, fairly dry, although a bit draughty; and our kit was first-rate. We slept on the usual "donkey's breakfast," of course, but it isn't the worst bed to sleep on, by a long chalk. And it felt real good to me when the "Get-out-of-bed" bugle went every morning before sun-up, and the Kanuck band made the camp rounds to the tune of *John Peel*. How we cursed that band!

Our daily work began with the usual before-breakfast breather—a brisk march over the hills, a spell of physical exercise, a pipe-opening "double," and then a free-and-easy tramp back to camp, soap-and-water, and breakfast. The feeds we used to take! I reckon the morning programme alone in the Army would fetch a double "lunger" back from the hearse door—if it didn't kill him outright. Dyspepsia disappeared from our camp, while as for stomachs, we grew to forget that such things formed part of our interior works—except when they reminded us in unmistakable terms that "Nature abhorred a vacuum."

The forenoon was generally spent on the parade ground, carrying out platoon and company drill. To give the reader an idea of the size of our fellows it is only necessary to state that in my platoon (No. 4) there were six men on my right—and I stand over six feet in height. I believe there was only one man in the platoon under five feet ten. They were not "cornstalks" either; they carried weight on top of their legs.

After lunch we usually went for a route-march, a form of training which was highly popular with all. On most days we did about ten miles, but twice a week or so we put in a fifteen to twenty mile stunt, cutting out the pace at a good round bat. Considering the state of the going (in many places the roads were simply muddy swamps) and the hilly nature of the country, I reckon we'd have given points to most fellows when it came to hitting the wallaby. Once I remember taking part in a platoon marching competition. My platoon won it by a short neck, but we were all out. The distance was just over eleven miles of as tough and dirty going as they make, and when it is borne in mind that we cut it out at an average pace of four-and-a-half miles an hour the reader will guess that we didn't sprout much moss on the trail. We lost a goodish deal of sweat that trip, but the messing contractor didn't look like saying grace over our dinner that night. (By the wish of the men the evening meal was made the principal one; it was always a solid, hot tuck-in, and the best preparation for a cold wintry night that I know of.)

For recreation we had football on Saturdays and—don't look shocked, dear reader!—Sundays; concerts and "smokers" on week-nights, etc. We rigged a spare hut up as a theatre and concert-hall, and it looked real good when completed. The stage was elevated, and fit-ted with kerosene lamps as foot and head lights; a nifty curtain, and the latest thing in brown-paper pillars painted like the front of a Maori *pataka*, with little Maori gods sitting on their heels, tongues sticking out sideways, and hands clasped on distended abdomens. The centre-piece was the gem of the show, however; it represented the War God, Tiki, chewing up the German Eagle between teeth like the tusks of an old bush wild pig.

Altogether the whole outfit had a decidedly homelike air about it—although it didn't seem to strike our English visitors in that light. But, then, neither did our war-cry, even when it was chanted in their honour by two hundred healthy-lunged New Zealanders. They did seem to appreciate the concerts we gave, however, and, bragging apart, we had talent enough in the mob to make a show most anywhere. We even ran to a trick contortionist and dancer, whose favourite mode of progression towards his nightly couch was on his hands with his feet tucked away behind his ears. Taking it all in all, we were a very happy little colony, and despite the mud, frost and snow, I fancy those of us who may escape the Long Trail will reserve a kindly spot in their hearts for the old camp down Bulford way. But, alas! our ranks are already sadly thinned.

As time went on our little force became reinforced by men joining up who had come long distances to do their bit for King and Country. We were a peculiarly heterogeneous crowd. There were men from South Africa, from the Argentine, from Canada, the United States, and even from Central America. One at least had fought in the Spanish-American War, and owned to being a naturalised Uncle Sam citizen. There were quite a few who had seen service in the late Boer War, some who had been members of the New Zealand contingents, others having gone through the campaign in one or other of the South African irregular corps. About 65 *per cent*, were born Maorilanders, the remainder being mostly "Colonials" of many years' standing. I should think we had representatives from every corner in New Zealand—and all *men* in every sense of the word. Men of whom Adam Lindsay Gordon, the Australian stockman poet, might have been thinking when in his *Sick Stock-rider* he penned the following lines—

I've had my share of pastime and I've done my share of toil:
Life is short—the longest life a span;
I care not now to tarry for the corn and for the oil,
And the wine that maketh glad the heart of man.
For good undone and gifts misspent and resolutions vain
'twere somewhat late to trouble—
This I know, I'd live the same life over if I had to live
again, And the chances are I go where most men go.

And this *I* know: a finer lot of fellows to be with, either in light-hearted frolic or the grim struggle in which they were destined to take part, I never ran across in my natural.

CHAPTER 2

Off

We sailed from Southampton on December 12, 1914, the name of our transport being the *Dunera*, an old British India Company steamer, I believe. The Canadians were no end sorry that they weren't going with us, and our fellows would have liked nothing better, for both contingents had grown to like and respect each other. However, it wasn't to be, and being debarred from accompanying us the men of the Western Dominion did the next best thing and gave us a rousing send-off. They turned out about two battalions as a guard of honour, and, headed by a couple of bands, we marched the two miles to Bulford Siding between a double line of cheering and hat-waving "Kanucks." They may have been a bit lively, those Canadians, but their hearts were where they belonged, and they were all white.

She was a rare old hooker, was the ss. *Dunera*. Besides our little lot of 250 she carried over 1400 "Terriers," many of whom looked as if they hadn't forgotten the taste of their mothers' milk. They were a poor lot as regards height and build, and our fellows could have given them a couple of inches and a deal of weight all round. However, they may have done all right in the scrapping, like many another Territorial regiment: one often gets left when one starts in to judge by appearances, and a weed many a time carries a bigger heart than a score of six-footers.

We slept in hammocks, and were packed in like sheep in a pen. The tucker wasn't much to write home about; still there was enough of it, and sea air is one of the best sauces I know of—when there isn't too much of it!

Our deck space was a bit limited, of course, and after dark it almost vanished, so that a chap was never quite sure whether he was walking on it or on Territorial. Then there were other things which made the going even more treacherous—and we carried broken weather right down through the Bay!

Our lot were quartered in the 'tween decks. At the best of times the atmosphere there couldn't have been much catch, so the reader can imagine what it was like when every inch was taken up by living, breathing (and sweating) humans. I don't like rubbing it in where men who have rolled up to do their bit are concerned, but the habits of those Terrier shipmates of ours were enough to set you thinking. They brought homeliness to a fine art. Spittoons (had we possessed such) would have been scorned by them as savouring of artificiality. Socks were made to wear, not to be hung up at night and looked at. Feet were intended to be walked on—and soap cost money. As for toothbrushes, well, they were all right for polishing buttons. The spectacle of a big, husky bushman cleaning his teeth night and morning was a thing they couldn't understand at any price, much less appreciate. "If I did that," observed one in my hearing, "I'd have toothache bad"; which seemed to be the general opinion.

They were great trenchermen, those shipmates of ours. Lord, how they did eat! I am beginning to think that we rough-and-ready Colonials from the back of beyond have girlish appetites as compared with some of the Old Country boys. And we like our tucker clean: we can chew hard tack with the next one, but we take all sorts of fine care that the cook washes both himself and his utensils. But those Terriers of ours didn't seem to care a cent whether the stuff was clean or filthy. Trifles like that didn't worry them. And the way they used their knives! Still, they were wonderfully expert: I didn't see a single cut mouth all the time I was on board the *Dunera*. Funning apart, however, they just ate like pigs and lived *ditto*. I don't like to have to record this, but necessity compels me. Tommy Atkins can fight; we admit it, and we take off our hats to him, but compared with the Australasian bushman—the man who fears neither God, man, nor devil—he is in many respects an uncivilised animal. True, we may have run across him at his worst. I hope so, anyway.

After leaving the Bay the weather took a change for the better; the sea calmed down and the atmosphere grew much more balmy. We were a little fleet of some five or six transports, escorted by a couple of small cruisers. Our ships were by no means ocean greyhounds, so we made slow, if steady, progress.

We killed time in the usual way—concerts, boxing, etc. on weekdays, and Church Parade on Sundays. Life on a trooper is about the last thing God made. I've had my share of it, and I don't want any more. I'm not greedy.

On reaching Gibraltar our escort left us, signalling to the transports to follow their own courses. We didn't stop at Gib., but pushed straight on up the Mediterranean. The weather was now quite summer-like, and all on board began to perk up considerably. The sea was a beautiful deep blue, the air had the wine of the South in it, the sun shone brightly, and its setting was glorious.

On sighting Malta we mistook a signal, and made tracks for the harbour of Valetta. Before we could get in, however, we were *shoo'd* off by the Powers that Be. We didn't seem to be the party they wanted, so we had to hit back to the old trail. Apart from wishing to see the place and getting a chance to stretch my legs, I had a personal interest in paying it a visit, as a great-uncle of mine, who had been a fleet-surgeon during the Crimean War, lay buried in the naval cemetery in Valetta. However, it wasn't to be.

The weather all through the Mediterranean remained as near perfect as they make it, hence seasickness was a thing of the past. We had the usual boat-drills, fire alarms and so forth. At that time there were no submarines down south, so we travelled with all lights going, both aloft and below. What with sea games, boxing, concerts, and cards the time passed quickly. Likewise our money. Faro and Crown and Anchor were the favourite card games; you could lose your partable cash fairly slickly at either. I have seen more than one pound resting on the turn of a single card. I reckon Colonials are to a man born gamblers, so it wasn't surprising that our available capital should be "floating"—in more ways than one. However, some one introduced a roulette table, and our cash soon floated all one way, the "bank" taking no risks and the "limit" being strictly enforced. Needless to say, the bank was never broken—but I fancy the wheel was.

Being in wireless communication with the shore we got an almost daily smattering of news, which was typed out and read aloud in various parts of the ship. Thus we heard straight away of the German bombardment of the Hartlepools. The Russians, also, seemed to be going strong, but we were never quite sure where, as the wireless operator made a queer fist of the names on the map. Come to think of it, it wasn't surprising, for they seemed to get most all of the alphabet into those Eastern front locations, and they sounded jolly like an assorted mixture of coughs and sneezes. It is easy to account for the illiterate state of the inhabitants of those parts; it would take them a lifetime to learn to spell their own names. So I reckon they just give the whole thing best.

We arrived without mishap at Alexandria on the 24th of December—Christmas Eve. It was a beautiful morning as we steamed up the Bay, and we got a fair idea of what the warships had to face the time they bombarded and captured the place. And right here I don't make any beans about stating what I think of that scrap. The town, at that time, was quite open to attack; the forts were old and crumbling; I am fairly sure the guns were not of the latest pattern; and as for the natives who served them, if they were anything like the fellows *we* ran across I don't think our jolly tars would lose much sweat in knocking the fight out of them. I used to read a lot about the Bombardment of Alexandria, but now after seeing the place (and I had, on various occasions, a good look round the old positions) I don't think much of it.

Once tied up to the wharf it was a case of get our coats off and set to work unloading ship. This took up most of the day, and a very hot day we found it. Some of the packages were fairly hefty and took a deal of handling, and I can't say we were over gentle in our methods of shifting them—at least the flying men didn't seem to think we were when it came to handling the cases containing their engines. Our old hooker was just alive with cockroaches, too, and regular boomers they were; some as big as locusts. As the various packages were swung over the ship's side the beggars kept dropping on us below. We didn't like it; there are nicer things than fishing for lively cockroaches inside your shirt.

The natives who were assisting us didn't care a hang about trifles of that kind. They weren't a handsome lot by any means, but they were a fine, stalwart crowd, lively and animated—like their shirts. They wore flowing skirts, elastic-side boots, and stockings that pretended to be white. They are intensely religious, always looking for *backsheesh*, and have no morals. When we started in to boss them up they didn't seem to know the meaning of the word "hustle," but, ignorant as we were of their language, we managed to enlighten them; truly, the army boot hath its uses.

English money, we found, would pass in Alexandria—with profit to the merchant who accepted it. Thus we were enabled to purchase oranges, figs, grapes, tobacco, cigarettes—in fact, 'most anything one had a hankering for. The native hawkers and bumboat men are a picturesque-looking lot of blackguards enough, in a comic opera way; they are to a man top-knotch liars, and invoke the aid of *Allah* to help them out in their perjuries. They are truly Eastern in their love of bargaining; also in their smell.

We left the same evening by train for Cairo. The Egyptian State Railways are, on the whole, not bad; the trains got over the ground much faster than I had anticipated: about forty miles an hour, I should say. The accommodation was good enough (no cushions in the third-class, of course), and the whole outfit appeared to be kept fairly clean. The carriages were hitched on to each other like a series of tramcars, a corridor running down the centre of each, and a couple of overlapping metal plates taking the place of the concertina-like arrangement used in corridor trains in England. If you got tired of sitting inside the cars you could always find an airy perch on the platform outside. To go from one car to another necessitated a climb over the platform guard on to the afore-mentioned metal plates. The officials appeared to be all Egyptians, and I am bound to admit they were as civil and courteous a lot as one could wish to bump up against. They knew their work, too, and didn't grow flies. The fares were reasonable—and soldiers only paid half.

Being a troop train, we travelled third class. On ordinary occasions, however, it is only natives who do so, whites going first or second. There are reasons for this; lively ones, too.

The old *Dunera* had been a temperance ship, hence our chaps had worked up a forty-horse thirst on the voyage. Now drinks were cheap (for the East) in Alexandria, so our crowd, being mostly old campaigners, took full advantage of what they considered a merciful dispensation of Providence. The bank not being too solvent, they couldn't all run to whisky, of course, and many had to content themselves with laager beer "made in Germany"; however, the bottles (and things in general) became a bit mixed *en route*, so they got, perhaps, even more fun out of the assorted brew than if they had all been sipping at the same fount. Our train travelled to an accompaniment of coo-ees, war-cries, bush ballads, and breaking bottles. It was a distinctly lively trip, and I shan't forget my first Christmas Eve in the Land of the Pharaohs. So far as I recollect, there were no bones broken, either, and not so very many windows.

We ran into Pont de Koubbeh station, a few miles outside Cairo, about ten o'clock that night, and disembarked straight away. A number of staff officers were on the platform, so we were fallen-in for a hasty inspection; and it was really marvellous, considering the amount of liquid refreshment that had been consumed, how steady a line was kept. It might certainly have been improved, but any little shortcomings in the way of dressing, *et cetera*, were put down by our officers to the fatiguing day we had had, plus the heat of Egypt. Perhaps the staff believed them. But it was a mistake to give the order, "Fix Bayonets!" when those weapons were already so firmly "fixed" amidst the gear we were burdened with that nearly half the company utterly failed at first to find them—and when they did succeed, the officers of the staff had turned to go: thinking, no doubt, that the climate had a lot to answer for.

We marched the couple of miles or so to Zeitoun, where the New Zealanders were camped, about seven miles from Cairo, passing on the way many soldiers of the Dominion, who were in a slightly "elevated" condition. One six-foot infantryman attached himself to us as guide, informing all and sundry the while that he was as "right as the *adjectived* bank!" He may have been, but he didn't look it. And those two miles were easily the longest I ever padded. However, we found our camp at last, and in the fullness of time our blankets and kits also, and, after doing justice to a savoury, if rather overcooked, stew, turned in early on Christmas morning. Later we were informed that the boys had fixed to give us a boncer welcome, but "*Christmas come but once a year*," and in the words of our informant, "they blued their cheques, got shikkared, and the show was bust up." We got to sleep at last, lulled by the dulcet strains of a Maori *haka* voiced by a home-coming band of late—or early!—revellers.

CHAPTER 3

Life in Egypt

Christmas Day on the edge of the desert, within sight of the Pyramids of Gizeh! The very last place in which I ever thought I should celebrate the festive season. And the outlook was far from "Christmassy": A big wide stretch of yellow sand; a rough, trampled track styled a road; a straggling collection of low, flat-roofed, mud-built native houses that looked as if they had been chucked from aloft and stuck where they happened to pitch; a few vines, date palms, and fig-trees, disputing the right to live in company with some sunbaked nectarines and loquats; a foreground made up of tents, both military and native, wooden shanties, and picketed horses; a background of camp stores, mechanics' shops, and corded firewood, closed in by a line of dusty poplars; in the distance the desert, a vast study in monochrome, the horizon line broken in places by an Arab village and cemetery, a camel train, and the forbidding walls of some Egyptian *grandee's harem*; overhead a scorching sun shining in a cloudless sky; underfoot the burning sand—and everywhere the subtle aroma (or "sense," if you will) of the East, at once repellent and yet attractive, calling with ever-increasing insistence to some nomadic strain that has hitherto lain dormant in our beings—calling with the call of the East. . . .

There was general leave, of course. Most of the chaps took the Cairo trail, those who remained doing so in nearly every case not from choice, but dire necessity: a week's pay at the rate of 2s. per day (once on active service we had to allot 3s.) doesn't see one far in Egypt. Our crowd elected to stay for dinner, and I must say the cooks turned out an A1 meal. The turkey was missing, *ditto* the goose, but we had as much frozen mutton, followed by Christmas duff, as we could find room for. The wet canteen lay close handy, so the beer (English, too) wasn't missing. The desert didn't look so dusty when we left the tables.

They are keen on the dollars, are the Egyptians. They swarmed round our camp like a mob of steers round a waterhole in a dry spell; everywhere you ran across their match-board stores where you could buy 'most anything, from a notebook to a glass of ice cream, made from camel's milk! They had the time of their lives, especially the orange-sellers. I have bought seven jolly good oranges for a half-*piastre* (1¼d.) more than once, but as a rule the price ranged from eight to twelve for a *piastre* (2½d.) Barrows or baskets aren't in favour with the Gippy fruit-sellers. They wear loose shirts and wide skirts, and by making full use of these garments one man will carry nearly a sackful of oranges—and at the same time help complete the ripening process. It paid to wipe the fruit before eating it.

In Egypt a man's wealth and standing is usually reckoned on the basis of the number of wives he possesses: when our crowd arrived many of the fruitsellers had only one—or one and an old one—yet inside a week or two the same johnnies were bossing up a tidy little *harem* of prime goods. So indirectly I guess our pay helped keep polygamy going—and increased the population.

Egypt exists by favour of the Nile. Outside the irrigation belt lies desert and nothing but desert—the Hinterland or Never-Never of Northern Africa. Except for an oasis here and there the eye searches in vain for a trace of greenery. A huge rolling plain of yellow sand mixed with limestone, and carpeted in places with round, seemingly water-worn pebbles, amongst which one finds agates in abundance; here and there broken and serrated rocks outcropping boldly in fantastic shapes from great drifts of storm-driven sand; a brooding loneliness—there you have it.

And yet in the Valley of the Nile what a contrast! The very atmosphere is redolent of fertility. Here is, indeed, a *land flowing with milk and honey*; a land which, give it the water, will bloom like a garden and smell like a huge *pot-pourri*. I have seen some of the best country in four continents, yet I never ran across richer soil or more exuberant growth than that of the Nile Valley. When one bears in mind that the methods of irrigation and system of tillage are those of the dim and distant past; that a metal plough is an object of mixed curiosity and distrust; that steam is not; that the fertiliser used (when it *is* used) once sheltered, in the form of towns and villages whose history was closed ere the Bible was written, the heads of their own forefathers—then one is, indeed, forced to marvel at a land which yields such husbandmen seventy-and eighty-ton crops of sugar-cane to the acre, and gives nine and ten cuttings of *berseine*—in the year, while carrying at the same time the mixed flocks and herds of the lucky proprietor. Little wonder, then, that the *fellahin* pray to the Nile as the Romans used to pray to Father Tiber—although hardly with the same objects.

The climate of Egypt was rather a surprise to us. True, it was winter when we arrived, but we had an idea that such a season existed in name only in the Land of the Pharaohs. The first night, however, made us sit up and think things, it was bitterly cold. Even packed nine in a tent with two blankets and a greatcoat over us we could hardly get to sleep; the tent felt like a refrigerator. Indeed, until we hit on the plan of donning our great-coats, and pulling on a pair of woollen socks, we were anything but comfortably warm. The days were hot enough, it is true, even in midwinter, but it was not till towards the end of February that the nights lost their bite. Before we left for Gallipoli, however, we found a single blanket quite all right; as for the days, they were something to remember in your prayers, the sun seemed to get right down clear to your backbone, and stew the stiffening out of your spine.

I saw rain only twice during the three months and a half we put in in Egypt; it wasn't more than an anaemic Scotch mist on both occasions. I reckon the average annual rainfall for those parts would figure out at about point ten noughts and a one. We were told, however, that once in every three years or so, the rain came down good-oh, and washed half the houses away, at the same time cleaning things up generally. But the natives take such things as a matter of course; being highly religious, they observe that *Allah* wills it so, and set about rebuilding their happy homes. I expect it's really a blessing in disguise, and the overflow from these villages of theirs should certainly fertilise the soil that receives it.

We were told by the local residenters that February was the month noted for sandstorms. Well, we ran across two—or, rather, they ran across us. We didn't like them a little bit. There was only one thing to do—get under cover straight away and stay there till the beggars blew themselves out. You would see them coming, for all the world like a big yellow smoke-cloud stretched right across the desert. Then it was a case of hop into your tent, fasten up the flap, and pray that someone else had driven the pegs home. If even a single one should draw—ugh! it gives me the shivers even now! Once I saw a pole go clean through the top of a tent, the canvas, of course, sliding down like a parachute and "bonneting" the inmates: I reckon it says something for the power of their language when we heard it rising high above the storm.

I have mentioned that we came out from England as an infantry company. Well, naturally we hoped to be attached to some battalion of the N.Z.R.'s (which stands for New Zealand Rifles). Failing that we reckoned on being split up and spread over the various infantry battalions. So it came rather as a bit of a facer, when we were paraded, told that a Field Company of Engineers and an Army Service Corps Company was required straight away, and given our choice as to which crowd we should care to take on. At first we were inclined to think it was a bit of a bluff; but no, there was no get out about it. Boiled down, it meant service with the Engineers, the A.S.C.—or our discharge and passage back to New Zealand. We didn't like this stunt at all, and at first some of the boys felt like shaking things up some; but, of course, no one held for going home, so they made the best of a bad deal and took their choice. I plumped for the Engineers; I had no hankering after the A.S.C.—or "'Aunty' Sprocket's Cavalry," as it was promptly dubbed, from the name of one of our officers who took on with it. ("Sprocket," I may say here, is not what he calls himself.)

We had already been through the mill as infantrymen: we had now to start in to train as engineers. It meant hustling some, for the time at our disposal, we were told, didn't amount to much. Well, we had made our choice, and although we felt a bit sore over being rushed, we knew it was up to us to see the thing through to rights. So we got into the collar straight away, consigned the war, the Army, and the New Zealand Government to an even warmer location than Egypt—and put in overtime imbibing engineering knowledge.

We had our work cut out, for we had to learn in the space of a few weeks a course that, in the ordinary run, would have been spread over more than the same number of months. But most of our fellows had done work of a similar kind, so it was fairly well into their hands. I reckon we had just about every trade and occupation that ever was in our crowd, from civil engineers, miners, surveyors, marine and electrical engineers, master mariners and mates, right down to shearers, boundary riders, rousabouts and bushmen generally. Even a few "cockies" were not missing. ("Cockie," by the way, is short for "cockatoo," meaning, in the language of Australasia, a small farmer.)

Hence we made progress like a house on fire, and the officers congratulated themselves on the kind of chaps the Lord had sent them. Indeed, some of the sappers could have turned the commissioned officers down had they chosen when it came to getting about a ticklish job—and I guess the officers knew it. So we simply took the course on the run, as it were, building bridges and blowing up same, digging trenches, fixing up and fortifying positions, and so on.

I think, taking all in all, the lectures were the most popular items on the list. Sometimes we had one every day, generally after dinner—which is about the sleepiest time of the day in a hot country. Snorers weren't liked; they disturbed both lecturer and audience. Apart from the value of the lecture itself one was always sure of a quiet, after-dinner smoke. Yes, I fancy those *pow-wows* ranked first in popularity.

Then there was bomb making and throwing. There is a lot of excitement to be got out of that racket—especially when you go in for experimental work. Some of our home-made bombs were fearsome contraptions. Most of us had quite a number of narrow shaves, and even the niggers, keen as they were to sell their oranges, wouldn't come within coo-ee of our mob when engaged in bomb-throwing operations. They knew a thing or two, did those niggers.

I almost forgot to mention field geometry. I fancy it about divided favour with bomb-work as an occupation. For one thing, it was more restful and distinctly quieter; for another, it was a jolly sight safer. You could sit down on the sand, when it wasn't too hot, and get right into field geometry without having to keep your ears open for a constantly recurring yell of: "Look out, boys! Here she goes!" or—"Duck, damn you! I've got a whole slab in her!"

Once or twice during our training we had a written examination covering the work, both practical and theoretical, we had done; and the examining officer smiled on us like a tabby with new kittens when he came to read our papers. Joking apart, he was more than pleased, and he didn't forget to tell us so. This sort of thing may strike the reader as a bit far-fetched—sort of blowing one's own trumpet; but if the said reader will pause to consider the class of men that composed our company he will be bound in common fairness to admit that I am not straining things too much. Colonial training, I reckon, isn't the worst preparation for most branches of the service; it turns out *men* anyway. And you don't run across illiterates in the colonies—even way back in the Never-Never.

Once or twice we took part in field manoeuvres—or Divisional Training, to use the proper term. For our little lot such things usually meant hard graft with the pick and shovel plus a lot of tough marching. The fun seemed to go to the infantry and mounted men—if there was any fun in the game. Sometimes we were out for only a single day, but it mostly worked out at a night and a day. Once we were away from camp for five days and nights. In all cases actual war conditions were observed.

I shan't forget the last Divisional Training we took part in. The idea was that the enemy, an infantry column, was strongly entrenched at some point unknown out in the desert. The attacking party, a division of Australian and New Zealand infantry, was to march out of camp at sunset, duly discover the enemy's position, and deliver a night attack with its full strength. The "enemy," to which my company was attached, left early the same morning, being given a day in which to select the position and fortify it.

Our luck was out when it came to dig. My word that subsoil was hard! In some places, graft as we might, three feet was all we could sink the trenches; we seemed to have struck the bedrock of Egypt. After messing up our tools badly and losing a lot of sweat we gave it best, contenting ourselves with raising the parapet where necessary, so as to afford the requisite cover and shelter to the defenders.

Our own O.C. was naturally anxious to make an A1 show in his particular line, so we prepared a boncer defensive position. We had stacks of wire, and we didn't spare it, shoving up entanglements that called for some getting through all along the line. It was understood that the wire would be plain stuff; but on the quiet, and to make matters more realistic, we shoved in a couple of strands of barbed—and smiled expectantly. We also rigged up a real good outfit in the way of coloured flares, and fixed dummy mines here and there in front of the entanglements; the latter were harmless, of course, but they sounded pretty bad when sprung.

The trenches were manned at the appointed time, the flares set, the mines connected up to the exploders, and everything made ready against the advance of the attacking division. Our chaps (the engineers) were spread along the position and placed in charge of the mines, flares, etc. It was slow work waiting; lights were forbidden, so we couldn't even smoke. It wasn't to say warm, either, and I reckon every man of us would a dashed sight sooner have been snug in camp.

Presently our patrols sent in word of the approach of the enemy's scouts, the main body having halted under cover of a dip in the ground about 1000 yards back. We had arranged a big collection of jam tins and similar alarms along the front of the entanglements, and it wasn't long until they began to play a lively tune in one or two places. We guessed what had happened: some of the aforesaid scouts had run foul of the wire, and owing to the barbed stuff we had mixed through it, couldn't get clear for love or money. We sent out a party to make them prisoners, and they were ignominiously herded in, protesting the while in lurid language against what they styled "a crook trick."

The first attack was delivered fairly early in the night, and resulted in a decided repulse for the enemy. Hardly a man reached the entanglements, for our flares lit up the heavens with a wealth of illuminating colours never before seen in the desert ("just like a —— picture show," as one of the officers remarked), and the explosion of a mine or two caused them to beat a hasty retreat. They didn't seem to fancy those mines a little bit, and had evidently some doubts as to their harmlessness. The whole thing was fairly realistic, what with the heavy rifle fire and the language, and both sides soon warmed up to their work. In fact, things got so warm that several lively bouts with Nature's own weapons took place between our patrols and some of the enemy who had crawled up with the intention of cutting the wire.

The next attack in force came off in the early hours of the morning, and after a long and fierce scrap the position was carried. In spite of the fact that they were under a deadly Maxim and rifle fire at point-blank range, those heroic infantrymen set to work in grim earnest, pulling down our entanglements and stamping out our flares. Time after time we notified them that they were all dead men over and over again, but they couldn't see it, and were disposed to argue the matter. Rifle fire, we soon saw, had no effect; however, there were plenty of handy-sized flints and agates lying around, and a judicious application of the same caused a considerable amount of delay and some loss to the enemy. I wonder what the umpires thought? They didn't show up during this phase of the operations—perhaps because of the reception that had been accorded them some little time previous, when both sides mistook them for an enemy patrol!

On being cleared out of our trenches, we retired to a new position on some rising ground, beat off the pursuing foe, and, operations ceasing, went into bivouac. Afterwards, the umpires gave out their report, and we felt good when it was announced that the attacking column had taken almost thrice the number of hours allotted to them in which to storm our position. But the infantry never quite forgave us for that barbed wire. The mines were also a sore point. And when we pointed out that it was simply realism we were after, their comment was brief and caustic: "Realism be damned!—look at our clothes!"

28

CHAPTER 4

East and West

Egypt is surely one of the most cosmopolitan countries in this old planet. It is also one of the most interesting. You will find all the breeds you want in or about Cairo, Alexandria, and Port Said—and some you don't. Quite a variety of languages, too, although English, French, and Arabic are most in favour.

The natives stick to Arabic, but many of them have a smattering of French and English of a sort. They are all there at picking up a new language, especially if there is money back of it. They will do anything for the dollars. They may have had souls once; but now——They have sold them long ago.

The newspaper sellers were real dabs at learning English. They used to visit our camps daily (like the "Orangemen"), calling out the most striking items contained in their wares. Everything out of the common was to them "very *goot* news"—although we mightn't think so. Thus one morning you might hear: "Very *goot* news; *Engelsch* 'vancin'"; while the same evening the beggars were announcing: "Very *goot* news: strike in Glas*gow*." We got to take this kind of thing as a matter of course, but it was a bit tough to hear: "Very *goot* news: Lord Roberts dead." However, as time went on their knowledge of English increased at a rapid rate. But it was camp English—Australasian at that—and when they took to airing it in the streets of Cairo things happened. They were especially disrespectful to the *Kaiser*, inventing fancy diseases for him every day, and prefacing each item with the usual: "Very *goot* news——"

One of the institutions of Egypt is the Bootblack Brigade. We struck it in full force at Cairo. No sooner did you step out of the train there than your ears were assailed by a shrill chorus of, "Mister, clean 'im boots." There was only one thing to do—let them clean them. It was no good trying to dodge those boys; they were out to black your boots, and they meant to black them or perish in the attempt. You gained nothing by bolting into a pub or restaurant; no sooner were you seated comfortably than they had you bailed up by the leg and their brushes going at forty horse-power. Even boarding an electric car didn't fill the bill; they just chased the car till it pulled up, hopped on board, and got to work. Swearing had no effect; calling their parents names had less—they were used to it. Let them earn the usual half-*piastre* and you could call them and their forefathers all the names in the Bible. You found yourself entirely in their hands; go where you would those Cairo bootblacks ran you down.

It is a gay old city, is Cairo. It is the home of Eastern curios, priceless fabrics, beautiful pottery, good coffee, bad liquor, donkeys, dirt, vermin, ear-splitting noises, and rampant vice. You can get as much of each of these goods as you like. East and West certainly do meet in Cairo. But they don't mix—for obvious reasons.

The Egyptian of the better class struck me as rather a fine fellow in a way. He was certainly intelligent, handsome as men go, and clean-run enough while on the right side of thirty. After that age, however, he was prone to pile on flesh and drop his chest lower down. His chief amusements seemed to be eating, drinking iced lemonade and sherbet, riding in big, costly motors, listening to the band, and admiring the Western ladies. In dress he was an out-and-out howling swell—a flash of the flashiest. On the whole I should say he liked and respected the Britisher in a lazy, good-tempered way; was a law-abiding citizen, but would never find the sand to stand up to the Westerner in a mix-up for the show-boss's job.

The lower-class natives were just a cut above the poor devils of donkeys they exercised their cruelties on. They would sell their own daughters to the highest bidder and throw in a wife as *backsheesh*. They were nearly all "crooks," and cheated you right and left if you allowed them. It was only a new chum who gave them anything like the price they asked for their goods. They hated you like poison when you drove a fair bargain and despised you for a tenderfoot if you didn't. They were as saving as a Cousin Jack, investing their earnings in donkeys and wives. I once asked a chap with a face like a Murchison black-fellow, which fetched the higher price: he side-tracked, but admitted that while it was always easy enough to pick up a passable wife, good donkeys were anything but common.

Taking them bye and large, the lower-class natives, as we found them, were twisters, crooks, and liars; they were (like most Eastern breeds) cruel devils with animals, loading their wretched donkeys and ponies down till they could hardly move, and then cutting them up with heavy sticks and whips till a fellow felt like putting the swine to sleep. I fancy they treated their camels rather better; camels are costly animals, and I have heard it stated that if ill-treated they have a habit of eating their masters. This I cannot vouch for, by the way.

I once nearly put my great toe out in an argument with one of the brutes (a native, not a camel), over a poor little donkey. I had only light canvas shoes on at the time, instead of the military hob-nailed boot. I never made a similar mistake again. However, I had the satisfaction of knowing that the unfortunate animal would be spared *his* weight for a day or two. In dismissing the low-down Gippy for the time, I have only to add that he is as husky as they make them, intensely religious, and works his wives and daughters much the same as the other animals he possesses. He is also a deal dirtier, and his washerwoman must have a lively job.

Before visiting Egypt I had the usual Western ideas regarding harem life. I soon changed that. I'd lay an even bet that the women of the East are, on the whole, quite satisfied with their lot. True, they have no choice in the matter, and have never run across anything better. Anyway they just take things as they find them, and seem quite content to graft away like billy-oh, while their owners lie in the shade and smoke. They are really only big children, these women, with undeveloped brains. The men have the education, seem to hold the bank, while the women are treated by them sometimes as toys to play with, and sometimes as wilful kids that have got to be either humoured or punished. I must say I never ran across a brighter or more cheery lot than those so-called downtrodden females.

We used to meet them everywhere, for they knock around quite openly, at times with their husbands, and again in charge of an elderly lady or two, of a rather more severe cast of countenance. They wore veils that hid their faces from the eyes down, and from what we did see of them were not on the whole bad-looking. They were rather fine about the eyes, and they made full use of those organs, even in the company of the "old man," who didn't seem to be overjoyed when he caught them giving the glad eye to a mob of khaki-clad Christians. We were warned not to return same, no matter what the provocation, lest we should offend native feelings—an order which, of course, we obeyed!

The Turkish ladies were as flash as they make them, dressed in what struck us as the latest from Paris. They used to knock round Cairo in big Rolls-Royce cars, and seemed to have no end of a jolly fine time. *They*, at least, certainly didn't appear downtrodden. I don't remember seeing an ugly one; they were as pretty a crowd as you could wish to bump into, and as lively as a basketful of jack rabbits. The way they used to smile and roll those dark eyes of theirs! It made a chap feel like owning a *harem* and turning Mohammedan right away. They were out-and-out flirts, and their veils helped them, being made of stuff like white muslin that you could see through. To our surprise their complexions were of the pink and white brand. They went in for plumpness a bit, wore high heels, hobble skirts, and ran to fineness about the waist. Their weak point lay in their action; they didn't walk too well (tight shoes, I reckon). But, on the whole, they were jolly fetching- and knew it. We were specially warned against those Turkish ladies. Poor girls! And they were so keen on learning English, too.

I used to like watching the Egyptian women carrying water gourds and things on their heads. I never saw one come to grief; their sense of balance was A1. It made a fellow stare some to see a slender little woman about seven-stone-nothing pick up a big *gourd* of water for all the world like a ten-gallon drum, balance it on her head, and trip off with it, wearing a kind of "old-man-you-couldn't-lick-that" smile on her face. I once saw a woman carrying on her head what I at first took to be a small hut; on coming closer it proved to be a large door piled up with all the family goods and chattels.

The man of the house rode beside the old lady on a donkey, encouraging her the while between puffs at his cigarette by singing an Arab love song. He had a voice like a quinsy-smitten parakeet, so, perhaps, that accounted for her staying power. And yet she seemed quite satisfied with this truly Eastern division of labour. They all do: ask a woman in Egypt why she doesn't make her better half (or quarter, or other fraction) graft a bit more, and she thinks you are poking fun at her; go one further and tell her that *your* wife doesn't do any hard work (which is a lie!) and she, if she can speak English, promptly informs you that "Engelsch woman one dam fool!" So there you are- where you started.

I used to read of the spicy and scented East, but it was some time before we struck the brand you find in books of travel. True, we had found a variety of "scents" in the land of Rameses, but they weren't the kind of thing you'd invite your latest girl to inhale—although they were all fairly "spicy," and typically Eastern. Cairo has its full share;

in fact, it bubbles over in parts, and yet it was in Cairo that I ran the travel-book's own particular to earth.

Reader, were you ever in the Native Bazaar in Cairo? If you weren't, take my tip and pay it a visit the first time you happen to slide Eastward. You'll not regret having done so. But—a word in your ear—don't carry more than, say, £1000 in your pocket, for you'll spend every *piastre* you can lay hands on before they let you go, and you'll blue the cash without caring a well-known adjective where the next cheque is coming from.

The entrance to the Bazaar is far from imposing. I toddled in by way of a row of butchers' booths and fruitsellers' stalls, to find myself transplanted straight into a scene from the *Arabian Nights Entertainments*. I rubbed my eyes, opened them again—and lo! the Grand *Vizier* bowed before me (with a face like an Adelphi assassin—but this by the way, for I don't suppose it was his fault). He named his price, I offered him 200 *per cent*, less; for a moment he seemed on the point of fainting from surprise and indignation, then, recovering, he accepted my terms and proceeded to do the honours of the place in the capacity of guide. An amusing enough cut-throat he proved to be, too, although just a bit too fond of talking about his adventures with the ladies. Some of his yarns——Ahem!

(Here in parentheses let me give the new chum a word of advice on the engaging of guides in Egypt. On arriving at the particular show he has set out to inspect—and often before he gets within coo-ee of it—he will find himself beset by an ill-clad and evil-smelling mob of hooligans all yelling fit to raise Lazarus. Don't let them rattle him, however; his game is to select the biggest, ugliest, loudest-voiced and most villainous-looking assassin in the push, make his bargain with the gentleman much as he would with a Paddy jarvey, then order him to "Lead on, Macduff"—and leave the rest to the aforesaid gentleman. There will be no further trouble with the other lot; the guide, if our friend possesses the faculty of reading faces, will see to that.)

I soon found I had made a wise selection, for a single glance from the *vizier's* eagle eye was sufficient to send the rest of the unemployed scuttling to cover. He didn't have to use his feet once; it was another instance of the triumph of mind over matter. I told him so, but I fancy he didn't quite take me—bowed almost to the ground as he requested me to "spik Engelsch as he no spik French moch well." I think he must have been the Prince of all the Assassins.

On entering Aladdin's Palace the first thing that strikes you is the narrowness and crookedness of the streets: in many places a long-armed man could pinch scent from a booth on one side, while helping himself to a silk scarf on the other—if he were not watched so closely by the merchants. Then the light is very subdued; something like that you run across in the bush, while everywhere your nose is assailed by the perfume of crushed flowers and spices. Look upward and you will see the sky a mere slit between the confining walls of the lofty, old-world houses; look around and you will see the wealth of the East in lavish profusion. In a word, you are in Old Cairo, to my mind one of the most interesting spots in Egypt.

Let us stroll down this close-packed double row of little window-less stalls that resemble nothing so much as dog boxes in a canine show. See that old fellow with the Arab features and dress, working so industriously at his clumsy native loom: he is eighty if he is a day, and just as likely as not ten years older. Note the speed and skill with which his knotted old fingers do their work. He is weaving a silk scarf, a beautiful piece of work, which later on may adorn the shoulders of some *harem* favourite—or a New York *belle*. In the next stall squats a native tailor or vestment maker. Opposite him a spice merchant calls your attention to his wares, just as his forefathers did in the days of Abraham.

A few yards farther and we come on a couple of young natives bus-ily pounding away with heavy steel pestles in a mortar surely identical with the jars in which the Forty Thieves secreted themselves—scent and *pot-pourri* makers almost certainly. Squeezing past a mild-looking camel, which we do not trust, however, we almost stumble over a couple of silk spinners, an old man and a precocious-looking boy. The spinning-wheel might have come straight from an Irish cottage. The yarn is passed through the interstices of the boy's small white teeth, the idea being to clean it of foreign matter, I suppose.

Flattening ourselves against a sweetmeat stall to permit of the pas-sage of a train of heavily laden donkeys, our eyes are dazzled the while by a glimpse of a silk merchant's stock in the booth opposite; hang-ing to the walls, piled in huge heaps, and lying around anyhow, are scarves, robes, and vestments in all the colours of the rainbow. What would that stuff be worth in London or Melbourne? Who knows? . . We turn the corner, dodge a cow and a goat that are being milked in the street, and find ourselves at the entrance door of a dealer in beaten brass and copper goods, Japanese ware, and antiques. This we enter, ignoring the protests of our guide, who would much prefer that our custom should go to the more flashy-looking store farther up the street—kept by his brother or uncle, most likely, and a first-rate house for buying Eastern curios and antiques *made in Birmingham*. You tell him so, insult the memory of his mother, and leave him to continue his protestations on the threshold.

There are many things we should like to purchase. That pair of vases, for instance, so beautifully chased and inlaid with silver, price £20. Or that group representing a couple of Japanese wrestlers, dirt cheap at £18. Or that magnificent cabinet—But our finances only run to two weeks' pay at two shillings *per diem*, so we turn our attention to flower-holders, candlesticks, and such-like cheaper lines of goods, enjoying the while a cup of excellent Egyptian coffee and some unusually good cigarettes at the expense of the proprietor. Shopping in Cairo is a slow game, so we kill an hour in the making of our purchases—and emerge with a balance still at the bank.

And now we come on a street almost entirely given over to the vendors of silks and ostrich feathers. What a wealth of colour! And how harmoniously the myriad tints blend with the flowing robes of the natives, the duller hues of the crumbling walls, rickety, projecting balconies, and sun-blanched lattices! Looking down the narrow thoroughfare packed as it is with a moving sea of quaintly garbed figures, suggests an ever-changing arabesque, kaleidoscopic-like in its effect. It is the East as Mohammed found it, a bit of Old Egypt basking snugly in the warmth of a truly oriental setting. . . .

We thread our way slowly through the noisy crowd of guttural-tongued natives, and emerge with something approaching a shock into the clang and rattle of a modern city street with its electric cars, resplendent automobiles, and plate-glass windows. Yet even here the East holds its own: you see it in the strings of camels and the numerous donkeys that dispute the right of way with the big touring cars and electric runabouts; in the open-air cafes; in the dress of the natives, especially the sherbet and lemonade sellers, and the hawkers of sweetmeats and cigarettes; but it is the meeting of the Occident and Orient, the commingling of the East and West, and the effect is anything but congruous.

Reader, I am not out to describe Cairo. For one thing, space forbids; for another, I reckon I amn't a boss hand at descriptive writing; and, lastly, you can get as much of that kind of thing as you want in the guidebooks. But I should like to point out three places you should really pay a visit to the first time you blow into the old City: the Citadel, the Museum, and the Tombs of the Mamelukes; add to these the Zoo, and the Hezbekieh Gardens on a Sunday afternoon, and you won't regret it. It is a gay city, is Cairo; a bad old city, but, above all, an intensely interesting one. You will there, it is true, find vice, dirt, and immorality flaunted openly, the trimmings all shorn away. But you needn't stop and look, you know—(you will, all the same). And *to the pure all things are pure*. Besides, when away from home things often strike you from a vastly different standpoint. You are out to "do" Egypt; you have paid to "do" it—then "do" it by all means. But take my tip, and exercise a wise discretion when writing to the folks at the old farm. Or don't write—just mail them the guidebooks.

CHAPTER 5

Day by Day

As time went on we grew more and more accustomed to our Eastern life. With the passing of the weeks the weather became warmer, until it dawned on our O.C. at last that, in the interests of his men's health, he would have to ease off work a bit in the heat of the day. So it came to pass that the bigger part of our training was carried out in the early morning and at night, the long desert marches in the afternoons being pretty well cut out. No one regretted it; those wallaby trots pulled blasphemy and sweat out of the chaps in about equal proportions. Besides, they were by this time in hard fighting trim; fit to go for a man's life. It was quite an everyday occurrence for the crowd to come into camp off an eighteen or twenty mile foot-slogging jaunt with all on, have tea and a wash-up, and then trot into Cairo to spend the evening. That shows the kind of training they were in.

But it wasn't *all work and no play*. We had amusement and recreation in plenty, between concerts at night, tennis, football, etc. on the desert by day. We even ran a gymkhana once, and played polo and wrestling on horseback—with donkeys as mounts. I don't think they enjoyed it (the donkeys, I mean), and some of the competitors got in the way of each other's clubs, and showed it. But the spectators were tickled, and I fancy the natives sized us up as all mad—or tanked. Add to this boxing, and Church Parade on Sundays, and you will .have a fair idea of how we put in time when we weren't training. The latter was the least popular; it was held out on the desert where there wasn't a vestige of shade. It's almost impossible to sleep in the full glare of an African sun.

As a rule we had Saturday afternoons off, also Sunday from the conclusion of Church Parade, besides an odd whole day or two, for which we had to get a special pass. Sometimes a fellow got the chance of going in to Cairo to fetch back a prisoner from the military jail. In this connection I remember forming one of a corporal's guard dispatched into the city to bring out a couple of chaps who had been run in by the pickets for getting shikkared and playing round some. The O.C. let them off with a caution—and a week later one was made a sergeant while the other got his commission! Still, they were good boys, so the fellows only laughed.

We were reviewed several times during our stay in Egypt—once by Sir Ian Hamilton. Oh, the dust of those marches past! They had the cinema going on us at the saluting point, but I'll take my oath they "snapped" more dust than soldiers. We were dressing by the centre—at least we were supposed to—but the line was hidden in such rolling clouds of suffocating desert topsoil, that it was a matter of speculation as to where the centre actually was. However, we marched as uprightly as the soft going would allow, mounted our fiercest touch-me-if-you-dare-look, and as the chaps actually in range of the camera averaged over six feet in height right through, I guess we looked some fighting men, and no error.

It was a day of tropic heat, we had been kept standing-to for over a couple of hours with full packs up, so our expression wasn't to say curate-like—as a mob of Gippy hawkers and sightseers who happened to get in the line of march at one time seemed to think, for they turned tail and bolted like a *harem* of scalded tabbies. At first it used to amuse us the way the citizens of Cairo stared at the Australasian troops; the place was simply dry-rotted with sedition, but after our chaps took it over there was jolly little talk of native risings or such-like. Of course, there were little isolated *pow-wows* now and then, but they always ended in such an all-fired jamboree that the tenderfeet *effendis* and solemn-faced *pashas* thought the bottom had fallen out of hell, and concluded to give the game best. Our chaps had their own way of tackling the beggars. And it worked O.K.

At another time we were paraded in hollow square and addressed by the Honourable "Tom" McKenzie, High Commissioner for New Zealand, and Sir George Reid, representing Australia. They had come out from London, and, needless to say, they got a boncer welcome from the boys. The Maoris made the dust fly and set the desert shaking with a big *haka* of greeting. Altogether things went off *kapai*, and I fancy the two representatives of the "Fatherland" (both real sports and white men) enjoyed themselves. Anyway, the men from Down Under were real glad to see them; and when addressing the Division the speakers soon showed that the pleasure was mutual.

It would be about this period that the Australasian forces began to be called "The Ragtime Army." I never knew who started the name, but anyway it stuck. Then some Johnnie, gifted with the faculty of rhyme-stringing, took it into his head to compose a set of verses dealing with our daily life and training in Egypt, every verse ending with the words, "Only an Army standing by." This title also stuck, and it was quite an everyday occurrence for the infantry to march out of camp to the sung and whistled tune of the "Army standing by." The fact was, that the fellows were by this time trained to the hour; they were sick of the dust, heat, and flies of Egypt, and were longing to be up and doing. They had had as tough a gruelling as men could be put to, and were beginning to ask what was the good of it all if they were going to be kept "standing by" in a God-forsaken hole on the edge of the desert.

You see, rumours were in the air; true, these "wireless "messages, it was proved, almost all emanated from a rather unsavoury source (the Anzacs will recognise the locality), but they travelled round the whole camp with most disconcerting frequency until one never knew what to believe and what not. And one of these rumours oft repeated was to the effect that the Australasians were destined to form the permanent Army of Occupation in Egypt. Hence the growing feeling of discontent, the constant grousing, and the daily lament of "Kitchener hasn't got any use for us; we're a 'Ragtime Army,' 'An Army standing by.'" But Kitchener knew what he was about. He generally does, come to think of it. He expected a lot from that ragtime push—and I reckon he was satisfied.

There has been a lot of rot written and said about the lack of discipline in the Australian and New Zealand forces. There *was* discipline, although not quite the same brand as that of the British Army. It is true they didn't cotton on to saluting as an amusement, and you can lay a safe bet they never will. But what of it? Their own officers didn't press the point, knowing the class of men they commanded. At the same time those officers knew that the rough diamonds under their orders would play the game right to the last man; that they would fight like lions in their own devil-may-care, reckless way—and, if need be, die like men, with a careless jest or muttered oath on their lips. I say there was the highest form of discipline in the Australasian Army—the discipline that called on a man to die, if necessary, that his comrade might live. Let the order go forth that a certain position was to be held *at all costs*. Was it lost? No—except over the dead bodies of the holders.

Has a single instance come to light in which even a platoon of Australian or New Zealand troops abandoned their trench and bolted? No, even when out of ammunition and unable to reply to a murderous fire. What was it that caused first one line and then another of those big Australian Light Horsemen to charge to certain death at Quinn's Post? Discipline! War discipline! The kind that counts. They didn't salute much (except when in an unusually good humour—or outside a big drink), even their own officers, but they would follow those officers to certain death—and well the officers knew it. They were just big, hard-living, hard-drinking, over-grown boys: not exactly saints or respectable church-going citizens, I fear. But they were white right through—even if they sometimes did go looking for trouble! And there wasn't anything on the Gallipoli Peninsula could show them the way when it came to scrapping. They were absolutely the grandest fighting men that God ever put breath into! You saw it in the square set of their jaws and the grim, straightforward glance of their eyes. But parade-ground soldiering wasn't much in their line, nor the cheering crowds either.

I think I have already stated that Cairo is a wicked old city. Well, it is. There are places in Cairo that I wouldn't take my grandmother through—places that would curl a padre's toenails backwards, or send the blood to the cheek of a Glasgow policeman. *Shebangs* where they sell you whisky that takes the lining of your throat down with it, and lifts your stomach up to the roof of your skull; a soothing liquid that licks "forty-rod," "chained lightning," or "Cape smoke" to the back of creation; the kind of lush that gives you a sixty-horse dose of the jim-jams while you wait. Real good stuff it is—for taking tar off a fence.

There are streets in Cairo where the stench is so great that the wonder is how any living thing can breathe it and survive; in comparison with which a glue factory or fertiliser works is *Attar of Roses,* and an Irish pigsty a featherbed in heaven; and yet in these streets—these cesspools—the painted ladies of low degree live and move and carry on abominations which are unnameable; things which the brute creation is guiltless of.

There are other streets in Cairo where the painted ladies of higher degree—the very patricians of their profession—follow their calling in an atmosphere of luxury permeated by all the seductive and sensual voluptuousness of a land which for countless aeons has been the home of the voluptuary and the pleasure seeker; an atmosphere to breathe which might shatter the vows of an anchoret.

There are houses in Cairo in which certain male and female vampires batten and wax rich on the proceeds of a thriving trade in the White Slave Market; houses in which wives are bought and sold like so many bullocks; aye, and houses in which, if rumour say truly, a man will sell you his own daughter—and not think it worth his while to witness the wedding ceremony!

Yes, it is a wicked old city, the Rio Cairo. I have a lively remembrance of a certain Sunday evening which I put in as one of a strong Town Picket. Our "beat" lay for the most part in the localities I have just been describing, and it would be putting it mildly to say that we had our eyes opened to the pleasant little ways of the Eastern. It was more than an eye-opener; it was a revelation. And in some ways I reckon it was an education. At the same time I shouldn't advise the prospective student to imbibe too deeply of that sink—er—well of learning. I can smell that aroma even now.

About six or seven miles up the line from our camp lay the native village of Maarg. I had heard that this was a typical Arabic-Egyptian settlement, and that it was quite unvisited by the troops, so I resolved to prospect it. Giving Church Parade a miss the following Sunday, my mate and I toddled down to Helmieh Station, had an early dinner in an eating-house there, and took train to Maarg Siding. The country we passed through was very different from that which surrounded our camp; it was all irrigated soil, hence the track wound through a belt of land blooming with flowers, lush grass, and magnificent *berseine* crops. Everywhere the date palm, the prickly pear, the banana, and the fig grew in the most prodigal profusion; everywhere one saw donkeys, buffaloes, camels, goats, and hybrid sheep revelling in the midst of plenty. The soil simply exuded fertility; tickle its bosom and the milk flowed.

Yet it wasn't worked. The surface was only scratched by an ox-drawn wooden plough, the pattern for which came out of the Ark. True, it was irrigated—as Joseph and his Brethren irrigated *their* selections. Here and there one caught a glimpse of a scantily clad *fellah* raising water from a channel by means of a rope attached to a weighted and counterpoised pole and bucket, or slowly turning the handle of an Archimedean screw. Occasionally oxen were pressed into the service, and kept to their work by women or children armed with *goads*. In such cases the water was raised by the agency of a wheel furnished with *gourds*, or *sherds*, attached equidistantly all round its circumference. The ox walked round in a circle, its *dexter* optic being obscured by means of a pad to prevent its entering on the broad way that leadeth to destruction—and, incidentally, throwing the water supply out of gear. When you bellowed *Ah-h-h!* like a goat, it kept going on its circular tour, and an abruptly terminated *Ye-e-es!* caused it to come to a full stop. It would rather stop than go any time.

We left the train at the siding, and bumped straight away into the usual mob of donkey boys and beggars. Threading our way through this lot we skirted a native *café* and store, and set out for the village situated some half-mile to the right front, the crowd of jabbering and gesticulating mongrels falling into procession behind us. In this formation we betook us through a plantation of date palms, past a paddock or two of vivid green *berseine*, and arrived at a flour-mill on the outskirts of the settlement. An old dame with a face like a gargoyle sat at the door selling sticky-looking native sweetmeats and Turkish Delight, while inside the mill was a crowd of women and young girls, some of the latter by no means bad-looking. When they smiled (which later on they did) you had a vision of ivory teeth, flashing eyes, and A1 lips and cheeks—the latter tinged with a nut-brown bronze.

Just now, however, there wasn't a smile in the bunch. They were as scared as a mob of full-mouth ewes. I doubt if some of them had ever seen a soldier in their natural—although I expect they had heard a lot about the boys. Anyway they just crowded into a corner of the mill and squinted at us like a bunch of half-tanked parakeets. Something had to be done. My mate solved the difficulty.

"How about buying the old lady out and filling up the nippers?" he said.

We did so, and in exchange for a few *piastres* received a fairly heavy consignment of bilious-looking lollies and Turkish Delight. These we straightway proceeded to hold up to the expectant view of the smaller kiddies. The thing worked like a charm: kids are the same all the world over. In a few minutes the mothers stole shyly forward and held up their babies to receive their rightful share of the unexpected windfall. Soon the whole crowd, mothers, kids, and flappers, were laughing and jostling round us to the admiration and envy of our retinue. They could not resist the call of those sticky confections. They had been seduced by a concoction of sugar and gum Arabic. We bought the old Ishmaelite right out and distributed *backsheesh* with a lavish hand, then proceeded to "do" the township at the head of a now much augmented following. I guess they sized us up as a new brand in the public philanthropic line. It wasn't every day that millionaires who sported five-*piastre* pieces came to town. I fancy *their* coinage was a copper one.

Maarg we found to be a typical *fellaheen* village, inhabited by the usual mob of picturesque-looking and untidy natives, half Egyptian and half Arabic; goats, donkeys, bastard sheep, and hens. It boasted a miniature mosque, a grocery and provision store, a broken-down potter's factory, a cemetery, but no sanitation department. The low, dirty-white houses were topped by the customary flat roofs on which the family washing (when there happened to be any) flaunted its shameless nakedness. The streets, carpeted with the freewill offerings of the citizens, began anywhere and finished nowhere—except when they led you unsuspectingly into the living-room of one of the aforesaid citizens. On the whole we found Maarg to be a really interesting place, and the inhabitants even more interesting. But they took some getting acquainted with, for at first every woman and child bolted to cover as soon as we loomed in sight, following at a safe distance when we had passed on, and stopping when we stopped. We smiled our sweetest: no effect. We purchased lollies from the provision merchant and started scrambles among our own immediate train: they approached.

Those scrambles were the limit. They began with the nippers. Then the flappers joined in. Next the mothers, some with babies in their arms, took a hand in the deal. Finally the men, their dignity upset by the thought of so much good tucker going into other stomachs than their own, joined in the general mix-up, and the show ended in a flurry of legs and wings for all the world like a cross between a ballet dance and a Rugby scrum.

We had a most interesting conversation with the mayor, or Sheik, or whatever he was, of the community. He proved quite an affable old gentleman, able to speak a little English. He didn't seem quite able to size us up at first, and was naturally curious to know what had brought us to his township. We said we had come on a matrimonial project (we thought we might as well tell a good one when we were about it; they are all liars in those parts, anyway), whereat he pricked up his old ears, scenting *backsheesh*. In answer to certain parental queries we informed him that we possessed a wife each already out in New Zealand (which was a lie), my mate owning to five kiddies, and I to a couple—the latter bit of information striking him as rather ludicrous seeing that I had just told him that I had been married a little over a year; however, I

43

made it right by explaining that my family consisted of twins.

If we had been objects of curiosity before we were tenfold so now. The market was well stocked, and had we wished we could have been fixed up with a tidy little *harem* each right away. It was a toughish job keeping our faces straight, while the goods were paraded before us and a full inventory of each laughing-eyed young lady's charms and accomplishments made out. And some of them were real pretty; quite as modest, too, in their own way? as most white girls. Not that they were niggers (except in name); the colour of a ripe peach would about fill the bill; and when you get that brand of complexion added to a smallish mouth and chin, teeth like pearls, a short straight nose, a low broad forehead thatched with glossy, raven-black hair (plenty of it, too), you begin to tumble to the fact that the *fellaheen* girls weren't *all* behind the door when faces were served out. As regards hands and feet they could give points to most Englishwomen, while their action was a treat to watch. I guess the Eastern habit of carrying loads on their heads accounts for their graceful carriage. They were a smallish breed; slimly built and averaging about five feet and a fraction, I should say.

I forget what the price ruled at, taken in a camel, donkey, and goat currency. The sheik's own favourite daughters, I know, had a top-market reserve placed on them. They were certainly the pick of the bunch. Like most native women they had a tender spot in their hearts for men of the sterner Western breed—and like *all* Eastern girls they admired height and weight. We filled the bill; modesty debars me from saying more. They would have shaken the dirt—er, dust—of Maarg from their shapely little feet and followed us to Gallipoli had we asked them.

We didn't. We tore ourselves away, saying that we would return to see them the following Sunday. We meant it, too—being both fond of prosecuting the study of native types of mankind. But, alas! the following Sunday found us on the sea, bound for the Dardanelles and Johnnie Turk. We presented our prospective helpmeets with sufficient Turkish Delight to ensure them dyspepsia for the ensuing seven days, *backsheeshed* their parents till they smiled sixteen to the dozen, and took the back trail, escorted all the way to the Siding by the united population of the settlement. I doubt if we should have saluted the general himself had we bumped up against him, we felt so good.

On the whole, we had a rather good time during our stay in Egypt. Our camp lay close to both Old and New Heliopolis. The new town was built as a kind of Eastern Monte Carlo, by a continental syndicate which, however, failed to obtain the necessary gaming licence. It is spotlessly clean, the streets are like glass, and the architecture mostly snowy-white and Corinthian-Roman in design. An enormous hotel, said to be one of the largest in the world, occupies the centre of a prettily planted square; there is a fine, showy Casino, and whole streets of beautifully designed buildings.

It is, in fact, a model little town resting incongruously enough on the arid desert, a bit of Monaco transplanted to the land of the Pharaohs. A close inspection, however, reveals the fact that a large part of the solid-looking architecture is a sham, most of the ornamental work being moulded in stucco. In this connection the natives will tell you that when the heavy rains put in an appearance (they only visit these parts about once in every three years or so) Heliopolis begins to moult—in plain words the outer crust of lime washes away, and the town bears the appearance of a fleshless skeleton.

You can still see bits of Old Heliopolis—the Heliopolis of the Scriptures. In fact, the modern town is built partly on the site of the ancient city which the Virgin Mary passed through. Your guide will point out to you the Virgin's Well and what purports to be the tree she rested under. You can swallow the latter assertion with a large mouthful of salt; the plant looks altogether too flourishing and full of life to have so many years on its head. The original Virgin's Tree is, I believe, to be found close handy—an old dead stump that might be any age. In the Virgin's Chapel adjoining you will find a number of beautiful mural paintings depicting the Flight into Egypt.

A few minutes' walk will bring you to the foot of the oldest obelisk in the world, I believe: an obelisk compared with which Cleopatra's Needle is an infant in arms. Save for the marks of Napoleon's shot which it received during the Battle of the Mamelukes, its surface is practically unscratched. It is the dryness of the Egyptian climate, I reckon, that accounts for the staying powers of these old-timers. Most of them seem to have suffered more during Napoleon's short stay than they did during the flight of centuries. I guess his men were pretty rotten shots. I often wondered how they came to mess up the poor old Sphinx's nose, or what they were actually shooting at. It couldn't have been the old lady herself, for if they had they'd have missed her.

Still, I shouldn't say too much against Napoleon and his men, for the bread we ate while at Zeitoun was nearly all baked in the ovens originally built by them.

During our sojourn in camp we "did" the Pyramids of Gizeh, of course. It is a stiff climb to the top, especially if you are wearing riding breeches, but the view you get as a reward is really grand. The interior is also well worth a visit. You'll find the inside of this big sugar-loaf to be as hot as anything this side of Eternity, and you can't help wondering how you'd get out if the top fell in. By the way, most folks when they speak of the Pyramids seem to imagine there are only three in Egypt—those of Gizeh—yet there are several dozens of them, big, medium, and little, scattered about the country. At one place (Sakkarra) I counted either fourteen or sixteen, ranging from little *piccaninnies* to the oldest one in the world, the Step Pyramid.

I also spent a most enjoyable day on the Nile, in a native boat—*feluccas* I think they are called, or our own particular craft may have been a small *dhow*. We paid a visit to the palace of Pharaoh's daughter (the one that found Moses). The foundations and lower part of the original palace are still standing, the upper structure being more modern. The river washes the place on three sides, which, perhaps, accounts for it being fairly clean and fresh-smelling. Little *fellaheen* villages, partly fishing and partly agricultural, lie scattered here and there along the riverbanks just as they lay in biblical days. We visited one of these hamlets (they are all much the same), and breathed the usual mixed aroma of camels, goats, sheep, fowls, stale fish, and stale native. I don't wonder that Moses went to sleep there.

I had often read about the yellow Nile water: well, it is yellow enough, in all conscience. But it is a noble old river, and it slides placidly along as if well aware of the fact that Egypt exists on its good-natured benevolence. Its average breadth near Cairo would work out at about 300 yards, I should say. There is no sign of hustle or flurry about the Nile, and if you live near it for a spell you'll have a tough job keeping in the collar, for its spirit is apt to get into your blood some, and you'll find yourself dropping into as big a slow-go as the slowest of the natives who pray to it. And you'll enjoy the experience.

When the bank was good we used to make a point of visiting the show places that could be "done" during the hours of a Sunday. Thus we explored Sakkarra and the buried city of Memphis; saw and admired the excavated statue of Rameses; tried to read the bird-and-animal writing on the walls (some of which was painted *over* 2000 *years* B.C., I believe—and still retains its colour); inspected the Tombs of the Sacred Bulls, and were beat to guess how in thunder the huge *sarcophagi* were got to where we found them. We also paid a visit to Barrage, the place of many dams and much engineering effort—not to mention really pretty gardens wherein one may picnic on lawns clothed with English grasses, and yet rest in the shade of purely tropical and sub-tropical palms and tree-ferns. Some of the chaps even managed to see Luxor, getting three days' leave for the trip. I drew a blank, however: the fare ran to £2 10s. or £3, and at the time I was dead up against it—much to my disgust, as I should have liked immensely to have had a look at the Fayyum, the Garden of Egypt.

Taking it bye and large I don't think we did at all badly in the sight-seeing line, from the Citadel and the Tombs of the Mamelukes in Cairo to the Pyramids, the Nile, and other shows farther afield. We sailed in native boats, rode in *gharris*, and bestrode camels, mules, and donkeys to further orders. I don't think there was much lying within range of our purses that we failed to prospect. It is a mighty queer country is Egypt, and I hope to see more of it "when the Germans cease to trouble and the Turks are laid to rest."

Before closing this chapter I feel compelled to pay my grateful tribute to the many French friends we made while camped near Cairo. They were courteous and kindly at all times, and in the case of those who, like myself, had numerous opportunities of meeting them, their warm-hearted generosity and lavish hospitality will never be forgotten. They treated us more like brothers than chance acquaintances, inviting us into their homes, and going out of their way to show that they at least believed in the permanency of the *entente cordiale*. We were brothers-in-arms—just that. Surely Briton and Frenchman shall ever remain so. That I know will be the abiding wish of every man of the Australian forces. I had previously met many of our Gallic friends and liked and admired them; now that we have had the opportunity of becoming better acquainted I embrace this opportunity of expressing my admiration and liking in the strongest possible terms. I feel that I could not do less.

Vive la France!

CHAPTER 6

"The Battle of the Streets"

I shall pass over the Turkish fiasco at the Suez Canal. Suffice it to say the thing was foredoomed to failure. Whatever hopes the enemy may have cherished of breaking through and causing a rising in Egypt were squashed by the arrival of the Australian and New Zealand Expeditionary Forces. With those forces actually on the scene it is hard to comprehend what devil of rashness and crass folly impelled the Turkish leaders to go on with the venture. Perhaps it was pride; perhaps German influence lay back of the move; perhaps some queer twist in the Eastern character—who knows? Not I. But this I do know: they came on bravely enough—as Turks always do—and were slaughtered like sheep. It was just a glorified shooting match. Poor devils!

Reader, have you heard of the "Battle of the Streets"? That isn't its right name, but it's near enough. Anyway, it was fought in Cairo, the scene being a locality much in favour by the painted ladies for residential purposes.

No one I have spoken to seems to be quite clear as to what actually started the scrap. One yarn was to the effect that a New Zealander had been stabbed; another was that some Australians had been robbed of a biggish lot of cash. Letting the reason go, however, there is no doubt that things were fairly lively in Cairo that night, and at one time it looked an odds on chance that the whole street might have been burnt.

I happened to be in Cairo that evening having a run round in company with three mates. We had got comfortably outside an A1 dinner and a bottle of light Greek wine when the row started. As a matter of fact, we drove slap into the mix-up in a *gharri*, and before we got shut of it the battle had developed into a first-class slather-up. The street was packed full of Australians and New Zealanders, with here and there little groups of badly scared *effendis* working overtime in their efforts to get clear of the struggling mass of grim Colonials, who, to an ear-splitting accompaniment of yells, cat-calls and coo-ees, were devoting their energies to an all-round wrecking and smashing game. *Crash!* went a wardrobe as it struck the ground with the impetus acquired by a forty-feet fall from a top-storey balcony. R-i-p-p! went the balcony itself as it followed hard on the heels of the bedroom furniture.

Hither and thither rushed the lightly-clad love-ladies screaming as only Eastern women can, and stopping only to hurl a bottle or other missile at some grinning vandal who ducked quickly, then went on enjoying himself. Soon the street bore the appearance of a West Indian town that had bumped up against a cyclone. It was a work of art threading one's way through it with all those household gods hurtling round one's ears. Presently the street was illuminated with a dancing red glare as the stacks of piled-up furniture broke into flame.

Soon a house itself began to belch smoke and fire, the bone-dry woodwork responding eagerly to the licking tongues of flame that ran lizard-like from doorway to eave, and danced merrily through the interstices of the sun-scorched shutters and blistered *piazza* rails. In a minute the lofty structure was sheathed in rolling smoke clouds, pierced with darting spears of a ruddier hue; the whole house was blazing fiercely, the roar of the fire blending with the wild shouts and cheers of the excited incendiaries as they danced a mad corroboree round the burning wreckage in the street below.

Another sound—the clang of a bell—broke on our ears as the fire-engines came racing up. Out came the hose; the police, who had hitherto remained in a state of "armed neutrality," endeavoured to clear a way for the native firemen. That settled *them*; no Colonial will stand the touch of a nigger's hand on his shoulder.

"Rush the adjectived, asterisked, double-starred sons of lady dogs, boys!"

The "boys" did so. I never saw a command obeyed so promptly and with such unanimity. The black police were just as quick to appreciate the general unhealthiness of the locality, and left with one accord. The firemen, bereft of their lawful guardian angels, followed. The hose was cut, and the engines were captured. This done the mob proceeded with the work they had set out to accomplish—the cleaning up of one of Cairo's cesspools.

Another interruption! This time from the "Red Caps," the military police, a little *coterie* of well-fed, rather pampered, and intensely self-consequential johnnies who were openly accused by the Australasians of suffering from "cold feet." Perhaps this was just a bit unfair, as they knew Cairo like a book, and knew all there was to know about their own special job. But our chaps could never understand why an active man of military age and training should remain permanently on a soft town job (as *they* did) instead of going on active service with the other boys.

Come to think of it, who could? And some of the military police I have run into have had feet like refrigerated mutton. They didn't join the army to be shot at. Not much! Which perhaps accounts for their zeal in hunting down the unfortunate Tommies who, coming home from the front wounded or on leave after a pleasant little spell of "killing or being kilt," may have neglected to salute an officer, to have buttoned up their greatcoats, or committed some other such grave military offence—running him down, I say, and seeing to it that the erring one received every single day of "C.B." that hard swearing could procure him. Such, in far too many cases, is *their* conception of soldiering. . . . And the previous sentence reads for all the world like an Irish bull.

All the foregoing by the way, however. The police behaved like looneys. They seemed to imagine they had a mob of English Tommies or niggers to deal with, but when they began trying to force their horses on top of the crowd they soon dropped down to the fact that they were up against something tougher. They were told pretty straight to go home and eat pie and not come meddling round where they weren't wanted. They didn't like being treated that way and showed it, so they had to be shoo'd off. At this they seemed to lose their top covering altogether, and, being armed with revolvers, opened fire on the crowd.

It was now hell with the lid off. A number of the boys were hit, which sent the rest fair mad. You should have seen those Red Caps do a scoot! I don't think they got away unharmed; one I heard never got away at all. They had been looking for trouble, and I reckon they found all they wanted. You don't shoot down the chaps from the Colonies and get away with it: *An eye for an eye and a tooth for a tooth*, is the motto of the men from Down Under.

Our little party now came to the conclusion that it was time to take the back trail. We could foresee what was likely to happen. Already strong mounted pickets were coming in from the New Zealand camp. We made tracks for Shepheard's Hotel, but found all exits from the scene of hostilities barred by cordons of dismounted men. We looked at each other. There were four of us, all six-footers and all at least thirteen-stoners. There was only one thing to do—and we did it. When the part of the line we charged had regained its formation we were too far away to make pursuit worthwhile.

The "Battle of the Streets" eventually ended through the combined effects of thirst on the part of the law-breakers and the arrival of strong pickets to the aid of the Powers that Be. There was certainly a biggish lot of damage done, and the natives who saw the scrap got the scare of their lives. But I fancy there weren't more than a house or two burned down—more's the pity! Had the whole quarter been gutted there wouldn't have been many voices raised in mourning, and it would certainly have been no loss to Cairo.

One result of the row was the curtailment of leave to visit the city. From this time on we had to obtain special passes to do so. Signs were not wanting, however, to show that our stay in Egypt was drawing to a close. No one regretted it; the weather was growing hotter day by day; we had seen 'most all we were ever likely to; we were in hard training, fighting fit, and were looking forward with eagerness to having a dust-up with the enemy. In a word, we had attained to that top-knotch pitch of condition in which we felt we must fight someone—or burst. Hence when the call did come we boarded the train for Alexandria with hearts as light as our pockets, and the determination to show "K. of K." that the trust he had placed in our "Ragtime Army" would never be betrayed.

CHAPTER 7

At Grips

From now on I fancy this "history" of the doings of the Anzacs is going to be more of a diary than anything else. I kept a rough note of things as they happened day by day. For one thing the diary style pins the various events down to a kind of sequence and insures their being told in the order in which they happened; for another it saves the author a deal of labour. This by way of explanation and apology. Here goes, then—

April 17. 1915.—Sailed from Alexandria in transport *A26*, otherwise the s.s. *Goslar*, a captured German prize. We had a Danish skipper and a Greek crew—a poor lot as seamen go. We were quartered in the forepeak, the quarters being rough, but on the whole fairly comfortable. We shared them with a healthy and mighty lively lot of brown bugs. The tucker wasn't too bad.

The weather was fine and the sea calm all the way to Lemnos Island. Had a *pow-wow* with the O.C., who read out aloud the general's orders, informing us that we should land under cover of the warships' guns, that we were to drive the Turks back, secure a footing, and hold it *at all costs.* Anticipated heavy losses. When dismissed went and made our wills.

Were met on the 19th by the cruiser *Dartmouth* and escorted by her till the evening, when a destroyer took us in charge and saw us safely into Mudros Harbour. The *Dartmouth* informed us by semaphore that transport *B12*, steaming one hour ahead of us, had been attacked by an enemy torpedo boat, three torpedoes being fired at her, all of which missed. A number of soldiers jumped overboard, thinking the transport was doomed, and were drowned. The torpedo boat was engaged by our ships, driven ashore and destroyed.

We arrived in Mudros Harbour, in Lemnos, on the night of the 19th. It was just crowded with shipping, and looked for all the world like a big floating town. Were informed that there were over 200 transports and 60 warships gathered in the harbour. Had a splendid view of the *Queen Elizabeth* as she lay quite close to our old hooker. The anchorage was simply alive with destroyers, torpedo boats, submarines, etc., both French and English. The French craft struck me as being a bit mouldy-looking, not so up-to-date as the British. You could always tell a French destroyer, she was so crowded up with all kinds of deck gear, and had a general Back of Beyond look about her—like a chap who had stopped washing and shaving for a longish spell.

During our stay at Lemnos we amused ourselves by practising boat drill, landing of troops, etc. It was no joke swarming down a rope ladder loaded up in full marching order—and it was just as bad climbing up again. One of our chaps let go his rifle; the rest contented themselves with language. No one was drowned.

It was while lying here we had our first solid day and night's rain, the first really heavy fall since leaving home. The temperature rapidly dropped in consequence till it became like early summer in England. Were told that we should find no firewood where we were going, and orders issued that each man was to carry a bundle of kindling wood strapped on top of his pack. We shall look like a mob of walking Christmas Trees when we get all on. Living on bully beef and biscuits now; no bread.

April 23.—Had a rather pleasant sail in one of the ship's boats to-day. Landed on a small island in the harbour and cut a big supply of green fodder for the horses we had on board. Found the formation of the island to be volcanic in character, as all the land round about these parts seems to be. Not much sign of water, yet the sole of grass was good, and the colour a vivid green. Plenty of white clover, some of what looked like English cocksfoot, and a plant that struck me as Italian rye-grass. Heard the cuckoo and the lark, and noticed some small green lizards scurrying over the outcropping rocks. *Thought* I saw a tarantula spider, but wouldn't swear to it.

Coming back to ship found we had to beat against a head wind. Our craft was lug-rigged, the sail something like a dirty pocket-handkerchief. She had no use for beating; there wasn't a beat in her. Tried to ram an outward bound minesweeper which refused to get out of our way. Minesweeper's captain called us names that may have been true but didn't sound nice. Doused the sail and rowed back. In the evening we watched the French and English transports and warships leaving the harbour. Rumours fill the air—the latest that we leave for the Dardanelles tomorrow (24th).

April 24.—Preparations for the big event. Told that the staff were prepared to lose 80 *per cent*, of the forces to effect a landing; also, that the fleet could see us ashore but that *it couldn't take us off again*; once ashore we'd got to look after ourselves. The fellows stroked their chins and looked thoughtful for a spell; I reckon they were thinking of the pie that mother used to make—or of their latest girls. We were also told that as like as not all the wells on Gallipoli would be poisoned, and that we should have to do on our water-bottles for three days. Three days on about a pint and a half! And biscuits *ditto*! We began to cotton on to it that it wasn't a picnic or mothers' meeting we were out to take a hand in. Were served out with a 2-oz. tin of tobacco between four men, and three packets each of cigarettes. Handed in our blankets and waterproof sheets, so will be going ashore as we stand. Very stiff fight expected, as it is fairly sure that the Turks will do all that is in them to beat us back. Wonder how many of the boys will go under?

Later.—Under way. All lights out and general air of suppressed excitement on all hands. Some of the chaps making a book on the event, and laying odds on the chances of the takers getting through the slather-up unharmed. Others tossing up to see if certain of their mates will finish up in heaven or hell! No one the least downhearted; all determined to at least give the enemy the time of his life when they come to grips. They are certainly as tough a crowd as ever got into uniform.

Landing expected to take place just at daybreak or slightly earlier. Creeping along like a "mob of thieves in the night," as one of the chaps put it. Distance from Lemnos about 45 miles, I hear, so will be there in whips of time. Funny thing to think that one's folks will be lying in bed sound asleep at the moment we go into the enemy, and never dreaming of what their men will be taking on. Just as well, too, come to think of it. Weather A1. Sea calm; nothing to complain of in that line, anyway.

April 28.—First chance of scribbling anything for three days. Been through hell—just that. War! It wasn't war; it was just cold-blooded butchery. How the position has been held beats me. But held it has been—and it's going to be held—at a cost! I wonder what the price of crepe will rise to out in Australia and New Zealand! Here goes for a shy at describing our amusement of the past three days.

It was dark when we left the transports off Gaba Tepe and crept in towards the denser blackness that represented the shore. The night—or early morning, rather—was still; everything seemed in our favour; not a sound welled out seaward, not a light twinkled in the murk ahead. Could it be that we had taken the Turks by surprise? Or were they simply lying low and playing a waiting game? Soon we were to know.

On—on crept the boats loaded to the gunwales with the citizen soldiers from the Dominions. Every jaw was set hard as agate, every eye was fixed on the forbidding-looking heights now taking form dimly as the east reddened and the sky became shot with lengthening spears of greenish-yellow. Minutes passed—minutes that seemed as hours—while ever shoreward crawled the fleet of boats, and ever plainer and gloomier loomed the frowning cliffs that dominated the Bay of Anzac. Back of the flotilla, away to seaward, lay the British warships, their grey hulls floating ghostlike in the first of the dawn-like couchant lions scenting blood. A sense of protection, modified to some extent by the stretch of intervening water and the ghostliness of their outlines, emanated from those cruisers and battleships squatting like watch-dogs on the chain, alert and eager. Our gaze wandered ever and anon from the forbidding shore ahead to where those uncouth grey hulls broke the sea-line. Would they never give tongue!

. . . We were close to the land. The *wouff!* of a gentle surf breaking on a sloping shingle beach, followed by the *soughing* of the undertow, came plainly to our straining ears. Back of the crescent-shaped strand, now dimly outlined in a flatted monotint of leaden grey, rose the darker, scrub-clothed slope, its breast seamed and gashed by *dongas* and watercourses, that stretched to the foot of the sheer bluff whose summit cut the sky-line 400 feet above our heads. As the minutes passed the scene changed. Sand and shingle took form and colour in the rapidly growing half-tones.

The blackness of the slope beyond merged into a velvet green. The serrated crest of the ridge grew roseate as the first of the sun-rays stretched forth athwart the fields of Troy and touched it with gold-tipped fingers. A newborn day begotten of early summer had sprung from the womb of an Eastern night—a day fraught with much of suffering, much of mutilation and death, but surely a day that shall live in the history of the British Empire so long as that Empire stands. . . .

Was it the surprise we all hoped for, after all? the surprise that seemed beyond the bounds of possibility. Were there *any* Turks there waiting to oppose us at all? And if so, where were they hidden? In trenches cut on the beach? In the scrub? Behind the crest of the cliff? God! were they never going to show themselves——?

Crash! Bang! Z-z-z-z-ip! It was hell let loose—hell with the bottom out! The whole beach belched flame and spat bullets. The scrub behind burst forth into a sheet of fire. Maxims—maxims everywhere! The place seemed alive with them. It was as if we had received a blizzard of lead in our faces. The physical shock was almost more than flesh and blood could bear. For a moment it seemed as if the whole flotilla was doomed—a moment in which whole boat-loads of brave men were absolutely cut to pieces and mangled out of all recognition—in which boats were blown from the water, smashed into matchwood and riddled from stem to stern by the high explosive and shrapnel fire that came over the crest of the cliff hot on the heels of the rifle and machine-gun fire.

Just a moment! Then the men from the bush, the plains, and the cities of Australasia showed the stuff they were made of. In dashed the boats—in anyhow, no matter how, so long as they touched Turkish soil—some bow on, some stern on, some broadside. All higgledy-piggledy, a confused mass like a huge dismembered raft tossed on a sea that hissed and spouted as its surface was torn by the never-ceasing rain of lead and iron. Over the sides of the boats dived and rolled those splendid infantrymen, their bayonets already fixed. They knew what to do; no need to give them orders. No time to form—no time to think. The cold steel—nothing but the steel! Off fell their packs; down dropped their bayonet points, and with a wild yell that rose even above the awful battle roar that made day hideous they hurled themselves straight as their rifles at the unseen enemy.

In sixes and sevens, in tens and twenties, in platoons, in half-companies—just as they tumbled out of the boats—those great-hearted fellows dashed up the beach and into that sickening inferno. They didn't fire a shot; they didn't waste a single second. They just flung their heavy packs from their shoulders, bent their heads to the storm, and with every inch of pace at their command they charged the Turkish trenches, some fifty yards distant.

Charge! I never saw a charge like it. It was a wild, breakneck rush, regardless of losses. Nothing short of killing every man of that magnificent soldiery could have stopped their onslaught. The machine-guns and rifles took their toll—but they utterly failed to beat down that desperate assault delivered by those iron-nerved men—those men who openly boasted that they feared "neither God, man, nor devil." In a moment they were into the enemy's front line of trench, machine-guns were captured, and the Turks got a taste of the bayonet that will never be forgotten by those who escaped. And they were few.

Just a minute of hacking, slashing, and stabbing—one minute of sickening yet exhilarating butchery in which no quarter was given; when to *kill!* and *kill!* was joy unspeakable—and those long, lean, brown-faced men with the square jaws and fierce eyes were up again, their bayonets smoking, and charging the second line of trenches with the same dare-devil recklessness. What power on earth could stop such men? Not the Turks, anyway. With imploring cries of "*Allah!—Allah!*" they abandoned their trenches and scurried up through the scrub, the panting Colonials straining every nerve to overtake them.

It is difficult to understand the Australasian character. He will joke even in the midst of danger, nay, death. He is, as a rule, a "hard doer"; and even his best friends must admit that he is often a hard, and fairly original, swearer. Nothing is safe from him when looking for a butt; very little is sacred, I fear, and his humour takes a queer bent some-times: which accounted for the behaviour of the landing force on this occasion, dear reader—that and the desire to inflict all the Arabic he knew (picked up in Egypt) on the fleeing Turk.

"*Imshi! Yalla!*" yelled the now laughing Colonials, as they followed hard on the heels of the enemy.

"*Allah! Allah!*" continued the Turks, and they put on an extra spurt.

"*Allah* be d——d! Clean 'em boots! Eggs is cook! Three for a l'arf! *Imshi*, you all-fired illegitimates!"

Such, with the addition of ear-splitting coo-ees, wild bush oaths, and a running fire of blasphemy and unearthly cat-calls were the bat-tle cries of the men from Down Under as they drove the enemy out of his trenches and up the hill, through the scrub, over *dongas* and gullies, right to the base of the sheer cliff itself, up which finally, all mixed together and sliding, crawling, and clinging like monkeys, scrambled pursuer and pursued in one loosely strung mob of panting, war-drunken men. It was the personification of grandeur: it was the apotheosis of the ludicrous. In a word it was the old reckless, dare-devil spirit of their ancestors—the men who carved out the British Empire—reborn in those virile youths and young men from that big-ger and fresher and brighter Britain overseas.

Meantime the guns of the fleet were pouring in a terrific fire, their shells screaming overhead and bursting well beyond the ridge. It was difficult at first to see what execution they were doing, and at this stage of the fight I don't think many of the enemy were bagged. As our chaps advanced farther inland the shells from the ships began to pitch amongst them, so their elevation was raised and their fire concentrated on the Turkish communications and on the dominating hills that lay on our flanks. They also tried hard to locate and silence the enemy's big guns, but they were so well concealed that it was almost impossible to silence them.

Once on top of the ridge our fellows paused for a minute or two to get their breath, then, as full of fight as ever, they doubled into the scrub and pursued the retreating Turks with unabated ardour. It was now an open battle, and except for the fact that the Anzacs were exposed to a heavy shrapnel fire, Jack was as good as his master. In threes and fours at a time the shells burst over and swept through the lines of advancing men, taking their toll all the time. The Turks took full advantage of the plentiful cover; they knew the country and we didn't. Now and then one caught a glimpse of a fleeing figure or two; that was all.

We had no field artillery to cover our advance, and the consequence was we suffered heavily, our guns not coming into action till the evening, and then only one or two had been landed. Add to this the natural difficulties of a broken and rugged country which we had never seen before, and the reader will have some conception of the task that faced the Dominion troops. It was next to impossible to keep in touch with each other, let alone preserve something approaching an unbroken line. Thus the fight resolved itself largely into one of units. Here and there isolated bodies of infantry pushed far ahead, then lying down they held on grimly until the main force came up and eased the pressure.

One or two lots got caught in the beds of deep gullies, were opened on by concealed enfilade fire from machine-guns and rifles, and died to a man. But they died fighting. One party at least fought its way almost to the Narrows, and then disappeared: not a single man returned. The rest pushed on and on, trusting to the reserves coming up and enabling them to hold the captured ground—those reserves that came in driblets only. The fact was that the men could not be thrown ashore quickly enough to reinforce in the strength required. Where battalions landed there should have been brigades; where brigades, divisions. It was just sheer bad luck. No blame attached to the fleet—every man worked like a Trojan, worked on without paying the slightest attention to the hail of projectiles falling around.

They were white right through, those boys from the warships, from the plucky little middies and the jolly "Jacks" right up to the senior officers. I pity the chap who ever says a word against them if any of the Anzacs happen to be within coo-ee of him! Come to think it over, I don't see that blame could be fixed on any one. The country was just made for defensive purposes; it would have required division after division to have been thrown in on each other's heels in order to reduce it, or to seize the ground to the Narrows and hang on. We simply hadn't the men. And the natural difficulties in the way of getting up such reinforcements as we had, not to speak of supplies, ammunition, etc., were nigh insurmountable. There were no tracks, much less roads; the guns that *were* landed that first evening had to be pulled by hand through the standing scrub; the landing parties on the beach were open to continuous shell fire, not to mention snipers- altogether I don't think there was ever such a daring or hazardous enterprise attempted in the world's history.

And now strong Turkish reinforcements appeared on the scene. Battalion after battalion of fresh troops joined the enemy firing line. It stiffened up: we failed to break it. Our men were falling fast; half our strength seemed to be down, killed or wounded, while the remainder were beginning to feel the effects of their tremendous gruelling in the fierce heat of a sub-tropic sun. Still on came the masses of Turkish reserves. The naval guns, especially those of the *Lizzie*, cut them up, but didn't stagger them. They took the offensive. For a time it was charge and counter-charge, give and take.

But it couldn't last; the odds were too great. We retired fighting— and in that retirement our losses were something cruel. Machine-guns and shrapnel did the damage mostly, but the Mausers took their share. Only in one thing had we the advantage—the bayonet. When we got to hand grips with them the Turks couldn't stand up to our chaps, who went for them with the cold steel like devils red-hot from hell.

No man who took part in that retirement will ever forget it. Overhead burst the shells, underfoot the dust rose and the twigs snapped as the unending rain of rifle, machine-gun, and shrapnel bullets *zipped!* and spattered around. Men fell fast, killed and wounded; every temporary stand we made was marked by little groups of grotesquely postured khaki-clad forms still with the stillness of death. Here and there one saw a sorely wounded man feebly raise his head and gaze pathetically after the retiring line of hard-pressed men; others (and these were many) limped and hobbled painfully along in the wake of the retreating infantry, till in many cases another bullet laid them low. Most of our wounded fell into the hands of the enemy. It was hard to leave them, but what could we do?

Time after time we tried to dig ourselves in. In vain! The line had to be shortened, else we should be outflanked by the enormously superior forces opposed to us. There was nothing for it but to retire right back to the ridge and hold the crest—or try to! Back then we went, retiring by companies and half-companies. There was no running, no panic at any time. When the Turks pressed us too closely we gave them a shake-up with the bayonet. In many cases men had to rely on the steel alone, their ammunition giving out.. Time after time the enemy drew back while his big guns and maxims wrought their will on us. He didn't half like the steel.

We reached the ridge, and, exhausted as we were, started to dig ourselves in. Our throats were parched, for we dare not broach our water-bottles lest we should be tempted to finish them straight away. Once a man begins to drink he will keep on. In many cases bottles had been shot through and the contents drained away. Others had left them with wounded comrades. For food we munched a biscuit— when we had time! There weren't many biscuits eaten until after nightfall.

We dug a line of holes, scratching fiercely with our trenching tools, all the while subjected to a withering shrapnel fire. The naval gunners seemed quite unable to locate and silence the Turkish artillery, so cleverly was it concealed. Lying down as flat as possible we scraped away, working frantically for the much-needed cover that should enable us to hold the position, if it were possible to hold it. At times we dropped the trenching tools—to lift our rifles and beat back the oncoming enemy. Yet it was evident that the Turks were beginning to feel the strain too. Perhaps they thought they had us anyhow, for their assaults began to lose a lot of their sting, and we were enabled to get a half chance to dig.

As the day waned and nightfall approached they came again, and we were hard put to it for a time to hang on. Charge and counter-charge followed rapidly on each other's heels, and all the time a deafening fire was kept up along the whole position. Then the brief twilight changed into night; the fire slackened off; the moon rose, and for the first time since early morning we were enabled to obtain a few minutes' rest before going on digging again in the attempt to connect up and deepen the shallow holes we had scratched into one continuous trench.

We stuck to it hard all through the night, grafting away for all we were worth. It was our only chance. Yet at times we were absolutely forced by sheer fatigue to drop our tools and stretch out for a spell. Sixteen hours of hard, solid fighting through a broken and hilly country, followed by a whole night's digging; then stand-to before daybreak, and all the succeeding hours of the second day hold the trenches against intermittent attacks. At night go on working at strengthening the trenches; stand-to again before daylight the third day—and from before dawn till well on in the evening of that day do your bit at beating off the enemy's attack in force with a fresh army that outnumbers you by five to one—*the* attack by which he means to seize your position *at all costs!* Just do the foregoing, dear reader, and you will realise what those Australasian troops endured. And do it (as they did) on a pint and a half of water and a few biscuits.

It was on Tuesday, April 27, that Enver Pasha launched the attack against our lines that was to drive us into the sea. All through Monday and Monday night our transports were landing fresh troops under heavy and constant shelling from the Turkish big guns; under cover of the darkness these troops were marched up and placed, some in the fire trenches to fill up the many gaps caused by the enemy's shrapnel and machine-guns, others massed in reserve at the base of the cliff. Yet not a man of those who had stormed the position the first day, and who had been hard at it ever since, could be spared from the front line. Come to think, I don't fancy a single one would have left it. The feeling had got abroad that the change was going to be taken out of the Turks this time (it had leaked out that the big attack would certainly take place on Monday night or Tuesday morning), and the chaps were fair mad to get a bit of their own back. They did, too.

Our position as finally formed extended along the very crest, or rim, of the cliff for a distance of about two miles, or rather better. Here and there deep gullies, or canons, ran into and cut the line, or caused the line itself to "bulge" considerably towards the enemy position. Such was "Shrapnel Gully," at the head of which lay "Quinn's Post," where our trenches had to be pushed perilously forward owing to the configuration of the ground. "Quinn's Post," in fact, formed the key to the whole position; it lay right in the centre of the line, and had it been carried the whole bag of tricks would, in my opinion, have crumpled up badly, and a big disaster might have occurred. When your centre is pierced it's no picnic.

To the left of "Quinn's" was "Dead Man's Ridge," held by the Turks, and from which they were able to snipe right down "Shrapnel Gully"—and, incidentally, our camps and dugouts. It was from "Dead Man's Ridge" that General Bridges was shot close to Brigade Head-quarters down in the "Gully." No man was safe from those snipers; they seemed to be everywhere—before, alongside, and *behind* our lines even. Hence no supplies could be brought up in daylight; everything had to be done at night when there was only shell-fire to worry about. Afterwards we got those snipers fossicked out (they met strange deaths sometimes!), but in the meantime our life wasn't anything to hanker after.

Now had the enemy only succeeded in pushing us over the rim of the ridge, nothing would have saved us. Below lay the open beach. We couldn't possibly have been taken off with the heights in the hands of the Turks. I guess it would have been one of the biggest and finest wipe-outs in history. Old Enver Pasha thought it would look jolly well in the morning papers, I expect. Anyway he had no end of a hard try—and to give him and his men their due I don't mind admitting that they weren't so very far from succeeding.

I don't pretend to describe that struggle. No man could. It was grit, tenacity, and gameness opposed to overwhelming numbers. A battle of giants. It was sickening; brutal—and yet splendid. Men fought that day stripped to the waist; fought till their rifles jammed, picked up another—and went on fighting. Men with broken legs refused to leave the trench, cursing those who would have assisted them—went on firing until a second bullet crippled their rifle arm. Yet still they clung on, handing up clips of cartridges to their mates, all the time imploring them to "give the sons of —— hell!'"

They weren't Sunday-school models, those big-hearted, happy-go-lucky toughs from the Back of Beyond. But they knew how to fight—and die. They were men right through, not kid-glove soldiers. They lived hard, fought hard, and died hard. And what if they did die with curses on their lips! Who shall dare to judge them, dying as *they* died? And it may be that the Big *Padre* up aloft turned a deaf ear to those oaths begotten of the life they had lived—or perhaps He failed to hear them in the noise of battle!

The Turks attacked gamely, like the big, brave soldiers they are and always were. Led by their splendid officers, they came on in masses, shoulder to shoulder, and did all that in them lay to rush our trenches. They were met by a storm of bullets that would have staggered anything born of woman. It did stagger them: they recoiled before that leaden blast that piled their dead and wounded up in ghastly heaps and ridges like broken-down walls—before that smashing fire delivered at twenty yards range. They recoiled—yes. But run—no! They charged, charged right through that hurricane of machine-gun and rifle fire—charged right up to our parapets.

And now it was our turn. Like one man the colonial infantry leaped from their cover. *Crash!* They were into the Turks. Followed a wild hurly-burly of hacking and stabbing while one might count twenty slowly; then the enemy were beaten back, and the defenders ran, limped, and crawled back to their trenches and took to their rifles again.

Thus it went on from before dawn till towards evening. Charge and counter-charge, till men reeled from sheer exhaustion, and their blood-clotted weapons slipped from hands sticky with the same red paint. I am not exaggerating; those who were present on that awful Tuesday will bear me out.

We were hard pressed. The strongest men in the world are only human. Loss of sleep, insufficient food, and practically no water, combined with the exertions we had already gone through, began to tell their tale. Our losses were also very heavy; and owing to the slippery state of the clay soil, following on an all-night of rain, our reserves could not get up quickly enough. Thus yards and yards of trench were at times empty of all save dead and wounded men, and in some cases the Turks effected a footing in them; they were always driven 'out again, however, or bayoneted to a man. Our fellows were simply magnificent; budge they would not. To capture those trenches meant the killing of the men who held them; you *couldn't* drive them out. And the officers were just the same.

But it was cruel to hear the continual cries of—

"Stretcher bearers!—Stretcher bearers to the right!"

"Stretcher bearers to the left!"

"Ammunition! Send up ammunition—we haven't a —— round here!"

"Reinforce! *For God's sake reinforce!* They're into No. 8! *Christ! boys, get a move on!*"

At this time we had neither support trenches nor communications—just one thin line, which, if broken, meant the loss of the ridge with all that *that* meant. We were also so clogged up with dead in our trenches that to make room for the living we had to throw the bodies out over the back. In many cases where our line was cut on the edge of the ridge these bodies rolled right down to the foot of the cliff. At "Quinn's Post" things were about as bad as they could be. There was only the merest apology for a track from the "Gully" up to the trenches situated on the very lip of the crest, and at one time when reinforcements were making their way in single file up this track they had to scramble in and out through and over dead men lying tossed about anyhow, while all the way, right down to the valley the wounded were lying "heads and tails" awaiting transport to the beach. It wasn't the most encouraging sight in the world for the fellows coming up straight off the transports.

In one place quite a little stack of bodies had been huddled together to one side of the track; there might have been eighteen or twenty in the lot. Owing to the water running down this stack began to move, and kept on moving till it blocked the track up altogether. I don't know how many chaps tumbled into that heap and got tied up in it, but eventually a fatigue party had to be told off to build up the bodies as you would build sheaves on a wagon. We had no time to bury our dead for the first few days—and in that climate you don't want to keep them above ground for many *hours*.

As the day wore on it became evident that the Turks had shot their bolt. The attack died down, then ceased altogether, and save for the heavy rifle and artillery fire they kept up on our trenches, we weren't troubled by them for some time. They had lost tremendously; the ground along our front looked like a heavy crop of wheat after the binder had been through it—either 4000 or 7000 dead lay there. (And they lay there unburied for *three weeks*.) At last we were able to get a little sorely needed rest. We had been pushed to the extremest limit of human endurance.

CHAPTER 8

Three Weeks

April 28 (Wednesday).—I am writing this in the shelter of my little dug-out, with the big guns roaring away like billy-o and the rifle, maxim, and shrapnel bullets pitching all round. One is comparatively safe in a deeply cut dugout; if you shove only your head up some sniper lets go at it. And this *behind* our own trenches. We aren't likely to die of *ennui* here, anyway—nor old age.

Heard that the Turks are mutilating our dead and wounded, but haven't seen anything of it myself. Strange yarns going the rounds that some of our chaps have been indulging in reprisals. *An eye for an eye and a tooth for a tooth* is the motto of the men from Australia and New Zealand, so if the enemy has been playing up in a way of that kind he'll get his own back—with interest. Wounded coming in steadily. Tried to get a few hours' sleep last night. Got one. Spent the night trenching, or sapping, rather. Engineers don't need rest seemingly.

Infantry holding the enemy all right now. Very big Turkish gun shelling the warships at long range. Doesn't seem to be making much of it. Heard that the *Lizzie* sank a Turkish transport yesterday. Rifle fire not quite so heavy just now. Heard that the British Tommies were advancing strongly, driving the enemy down on us. Just had orders to go on trenching at "Quinn's Post" tonight, advancing new saps and making a new advanced fire trench. Raining hard, a cold rain. No coat or blanket. Sure to be pretty miserable.

29th.—Came back to dugout at 1.30 a.m., very wet, very cold, very miserable. All sticky with mud. Got some sleep.

Weather cleared up later. Battle still going on, we holding the enemy safely. Went on sapping at "Quinn's," in four-hour-shifts. Very lively and "jumpy" work—enemy crawling up at dark and firing at fifteen to twenty feet range. Periscopes now being used, made in most cases from glasses cut from large mirrors taken from the ships. These periscopes don't last many hours at this part of the line, as a rule, and many nasty scalp wounds have been received through the glass being shattered by rifle fire. We have had to make them as small as possible- simply a lath with two small pieces of mirror about two inches by one. In some cases, even, a walking-stick with the centre cut out has been used with good results. Miss my overcoat and blanket greatly, the nights being cold. Haven't seen them since we discarded our packs at the landing.

30th. (Friday).—Still the same: battle going on. Sapping continued under difficulties. Stench from enemy's dead lying near the trenches very bad. Fed up with continuous sapping work. Tucker improving a bit. No mail yet arrived. Heard that Goorkhas had landed to assist us. Removed to new readymade dugouts further up the hill. Came back again on hearing that the late owner had been shot while lying in it. Message of congratulation from Lord Kitchener to Colonial troops. British Tommies reported to be advancing strongly, and due to join us tomorrow night. First bombs thrown into our trenches today—the cricket-ball variety fitted with time-fuses. We amused ourselves by making "catches" of these bombs and slinging them back into the Turks. It was lively work, and certainly exciting. I'd much rather play cricket on the Auckland Domain, however. RUM tonight the first is- sue since landing. It went down slick.

May 1 (Saturday).—Sapping: still sapping. Getting quite close to enemy, their nearest trench being now only about twenty feet distant. Plenty of Turkish bombs to enliven the time. One I picked up yes- terday and pulled the fuse out of was sent down to headquarters for inspection. On my asking to have it back—I thought of making an ink-bottle out of it, or a spittoon—I was informed that it was now Government property, but that I might *as a favour* get it back again. Shan't let the next one I get hold of fall into the hands of the Gov- ernment! Turks attacked our right flank in force, but beaten off by Australians after suffering heavy loss.

Our machine-guns simply mowed them down in hundreds. Things looked bad for a bit as the enemy shrapnel got well home into the open ditch that is supposed to be a trench, and our losses were heavy. Also, some fresh troops (not Anzacs, thank heaven!) sent up to help our fellows didn't play the game, letting the Australians down badly.

Why the dickens do they enlist boys of seventeen in some of the Home corps? They are only in the way when it comes to cold-blooded bayonet work.

Some of our fellows are now partially deaf owing to the all-fired row that goes on day and night. Changed camp today, shifting to other side of "Shrapnel Gully," about a quarter of a mile away from "Quinn's." Made a boss dugout for four—myself and three mates. While eating dinner a piece of shell as large as my hand (No. 11 in gloves—when I wear them!) bumped straight into our happy home, just grazing ——'s back. Made ourselves fairly snug with sandbags, etc. Have now got a great-coat (late owner past caring for such things), but no blankets. Got our first whole night's sleep last night since landing, rather broken owing to unusually cold night following extremely hot day. Snipers very busy; one said to have killed over a dozen of our chaps today down at a water-hole in the "Gully."

May 2.—Fight still going on: 8th day of it. Shell fire not so heavy, but rifles talking away as merrily as ever. Very trying in trenches, owing to stench from dead men. Read the following scrawled in blue pencil on a cross made from biscuit-box wood just outside our camp: "*In loving memory of 29 brave soldiers of the King.*" We are living practically on a big graveyard. Our dead are buried anywhere and everywhere—even *in* the trenches. It takes a lot of getting to like. Had a boncer breakfast this morning, firewood being fairly plentiful. Haven't had a wash, my clothes or boots off, since we landed eight days ago. Wonder what I look like! Made a road for mules from valley up to firing line, following a winding course. Came back to camp and heard that a big general advance is to take place tonight, commencing at 7 p.m. My section is to be divided into two half-sections, each under command of a non-com., and appointed to a separate unit. My party appointed to the 16th Battalion, Australian Infantry. Sure to be a hot picnic. Wonder how many of us will draw rations tomorrow!

May 3.—Am back in camp again with a smack in the right shoulder and a useless right arm—and jolly glad to be back, too. Am the only tenant of our dugout, my three chums being knocked over—all seriously wounded. Can just manage to write.

We had a crook spin. The big guns of the ships and the shore batteries started the ball by shelling the enemy heavily and driving him from his front trenches with some loss. We followed the infantry to the attack at dusk, advancing up a dark and evil-looking gully or *nullah,* the track being only fit for amphibious monkeys to follow, and so narrow that single file had to be adopted. We didn't enjoy ourselves a little bit, as added to the natural difficulties of the passage—we were up to the thighs in mud and water one minute and scrambling over roots, branches, and rocks the next, all in pitch darkness—we were sniped at point-blank range all the way, losing several men. At last, after a very trying time, we gained the top and found that the leading companies of infantry had carried the position and were engaged in digging themselves in under one of the hottest fires I ever ran up against.

Our little half-section of about eighteen men were ordered to spread themselves along the line, their duties being to advise and assist the infantry. We did so, and at once men began to fall. The Turks were only about fifty yards away, and although it was dark they could see our chaps fairly well against the background of stars. In a few minutes half our lot were down, I myself being put out of action by a bullet glancing off a pick and getting me in the right shoulder. At the same instant my water-bottle was shot through and the rifle blown from my hand. It wasn't at all a healthy climate. It was just a shambles. Men were lying killed and wounded as thick as sardines in a tin. I remember apologising to a poor chap for treading on his face. But he didn't mind—being dead.

Although my wound was only slight, it settled me for doing any more work, so I was sent back with a message to the O.C. in camp. I shan't forget that trip in a hurry. Owing to having to make a detour to avoid the reinforcements that were coming up, I cut across the back trail without knowing it, and almost walked into the Turks, who were out on a flanking game. One son of a gun tickled the back of my neck with a bullet, and another put one so close to my ear that I felt the organ to make sure it was still hanging to my head. That was good enough for me; I wasn't greedy; so I just ducked and ran, never stopping till I had to —— head down in three feet of mud at the bottom of a ten-foot *donga*! However, I got my bearings at last, hit the trail, and staggered into camp, more dead than alive, at about midnight. Delivered my message, had my wound dressed, and after a *pannikin* of tea turned in and had a smoke and an hour or two of sleep. Shoulder hurt a bit.

The captured position was held all day, but owing to being commanded by some rising ground on which the Turks were strongly entrenched and from which they were able to enfilade our chaps, it was abandoned at dark. Hard lines after the heavy losses. But life is cheap here. Heavy firing towards evening. Stayed in my dug-out smoking and nursing my arm.

May 4.—Very heavy firing all along the line most of last night. Distant bombardment by fleet heard. Stayed in camp all morning, but went up to "Quinn's" in the afternoon and supervised infantrymen sapping. Very short of engineers now. My section is just about wiped out. Enemy threw in a regular cloud of bombs, then attacked strongly. They succeeded in getting a footing in the front line trenches, and some hard hand-to-hand bayonet fighting had to be put in before they were cleaned up. Shoulder won't be "fit" for some time; however, I can always boss up others although doing a loaf myself. Had a very "scratch" tea tonight.

May 5.—Up to sap again at 3 a.m., and sat rifle in hand on a cartridge-box for four solid (and weary) hours keeping guard. Turks only a few yards off. If one had showed his nose over the parapet I doubt if I could have raised the rifle to my shoulder; however, the working party didn't know that. Nothing very lively happened. Sap head ran into a dead Turk, who was so tied up in the scrub that he couldn't be shoved to one side except at great risk. Only one thing to do: we sapped through him. It wasn't the nicest job in the world, seeing the time he'd lain there. Came back to poor breakfast. Could have done with a "go" of rum. Didn't get any.

In the afternoon bossed up a whole company of London infantrymen at road-making. There is plenty of variety in the engineering line I find. My company certainly didn't know how to go about the job they had taken in hand, and they had never even heard of a corduroy road, while their ideas on the question of drainage would have shocked Noah. Their officers thought they knew all there was to know, but really didn't know enough to know how little they did know. I had a slight difference of opinion with those officers. I got my own way.

The country here is rather pretty—deep gullies and canons with high hills clothed with dwarf oak (we called it holly) and firs; in the gullies one runs across the arbutus, the flowering thorn, a kind of laurel, and a wood that resembles the New Zealand *karaka*. Wild flowers bloom in profusion; my dugout is gay with a little pink rambler rose that threatens to engulf it in its tendrils. The growth is rapid. We have evidently struck the right time of year for visiting Gallipoli. In a way the Peninsula reminds me of parts of the North Island of New

Zealand.

In the way of bird and animal life there are larks, doves, pigeons, hawks, turkeys, cuckoos, and tortoises. The latter animals caused our sentries many anxious moments. I shouldn't care to calculate how many tortoises were "halted," nor how many were shot at. They were big fellows as tortoises go, and when a chap got a squint of one mooching along the skyline in the moonlight, it was all the odds to a tin-tack he let go at it.

In the insect line we could count quite a tidy little collection. We had flies by the hundred billion. They were everywhere, from the heaps of dead to the cook's pots. Put jam on a biscuit and it was always a sprint to your mouth between you and the flies, the event usually ending in a dead heat. There were other insects not quite so plentiful as the flies, but even fonder of our company—at least, they stuck close to us; they're not usually named before ladies, except in the pulpit.

We had snakes, scorpions, centipedes, and big hairy tarantula spiders; and when they elected to drop into the trenches things got fairly lively. We liked them just about as much as they liked us. A state of war existed between us: we took no prisoners.

—— AND (a very big "and") *there is gold on the Gallipoli Peninsula.* There is. It's there—for I myself panned off the dirt and found the colour! I know the spot, and some day, perhaps, I'll have a try for the big seam. I have a fairly good idea——But that's another tale.

There are other things in our trenches that we don't care over-much to have as company. Maggots—maggots crawling in battalions about a chap's feet and dropping from the sides of the trench down his neck. Maggots from the dead! You can't sit down hardly without flattening a dozen or two out. It's bad for one's uniform. Something will have to be done, or we'll all be down with disease. It's a good job we were all inoculated against enteric, anyway. The smell is worse than a glue factory. We have dead Turks right on our very parapets. Only this morning a bullet pitched into one lying close handy, and the putrid matter (of the consistency of porridge) was "spattered "right over us. They say you can get used to anything. Well, maybe so. But it's hard to get used to that. No news yet, and no way of sending any.

Later.—First part of a mail arrived at last. Two letters for me. Am going to try to get letters sent off; they will be strictly censored, of course. The sergeant of my section killed today—a really nice fellow and a general favourite. I'll soon have no chums left at all. Enemy is now using explosive bullets. I have seen their effects.

Driven out of sap every time we entered it by bombs. One burst within three feet of me without doing any harm. Firing going on as usual. Managed to get a change of socks today. Needed them. Rumoured that the British or the Turks have presented an ultimatum, calling on one or other to surrender within twenty-four hours—no one seems to know which. Also that the French have taken a big fort at the Narrows. Air full of rumours—and projectiles. Big guns almost splitting the drum of my ear as I write. Very heavy Maxim and rifle fire this evening. Quite sick of it all; the Turks take a lot of beating. Weather beautiful; sea calm and of an azure blue colour. Rum issued tonight. Big event. Things looked brighter afterwards.

May 6.—Heavy cannonade, but lighter rifle fire. Lots of bombs. Fellows getting quite deaf. Was down at beach today. Navy men very busy landing stores, etc. Officers (Navy) very fine fellows, and both they and their men swear by our chaps. No side or laddy-da about the officers. One—a lieutenant—informed me that our fellows were born fighters: "But you want to give them plenty to do," he went on; "for when they're not fighting they're looking for trouble." Afterwards I overheard him describing the landing to a newcomer. "They're not soldiers," he finished up, "—— they're not men! They're just wild devils let loose from hell! The instant the boats grounded over they went, head first, came up with fixed bayonets, and rushed those machine-guns like runaway steam-engines! It was the most reckless, grandest slap-dash charge that I or any other man ever witnessed. Oh, they're beauties to scrap! And their vocabulary would raise your hair!"

May 7.—Weather still beautiful. Position just the same. Fire from all arms still going on. Enemy sapping in line with us. More of my section laid out; only a few left. Being reinforced by volunteers from our mounted crowd—drivers, etc.

May 8.—Heavy fire all night. Fancy considerable waste of ammunition. Rather quiet day. Some artillery fire from enemy trying to locate our guns, which are well hidden. Mail supposed to come in tomorrow. Hope so, as many letters are due. Posted a letter myself today—in a haversack hanging to a bush. Hope it goes all right. Rum tonight. Very welcome, but short ration. I wonder why?

May 9.—Very quiet night, with occasional bursts of rifle fire. Enemy tried hard with his guns for one of our batteries this morning, but failed to get it. Notice posted that British warships have forced the Narrows and are in the Sea of Marmora. This should hasten the end. Hope so, as we are all fed up with sticking to the trenches here. Rumoured that the Russians are in the Bosphorus: don't believe it. Heavy, distant cannonade last two days and nights. Fleet, I suppose. As I write hardly a shot being fired. Arm still queer. Got a short rifle today in place of the old long one I selected. (Prefer long rifle for good shooting, sniping, etc., but short one better for the trenches.) There is a history attached to the one I have now. It was picked up just outside a new sap by one of our chaps, and when found the bayonet was fixed and a single shot had been fired, the cartridge case still remaining in the breech. A dead Australian was lying beside it.

Memorable event: had a shave today, the first since leaving the transport. The razor was a borrowed one; my beard was like a mop. Both suffered.

Was detailed as one of party sent to supervise infantry digging trenches. Went out at 8 p.m. and came off at midnight. Did nothing but lie about and get miserably cold, as I had no great-coat with me. Infantry made another attack on position they captured last Sunday and retired from. Carried it again—and again retired, owing, it is said, to lack of reinforcements at the critical moment. Truth is, it is almost impossible to bring up reserves quickly enough owing to the nature of the country. Hard lines, all the same, considering what it costs to capture these entrenched positions.

May 10.—Fairly quiet. Artillery still throwing shrapnel over our camp and right down to beach. Did another four hours today—from 8 a.m. till 12 noon. To go out at 8 p.m. again. Tobacco and cigarettes issued today, the latter in bad condition—very mouldy. Went out from 8 till 12 midnight to fix a pump and deepen a well. Had no tools, it was pitch dark, dare not light even a match, so did nothing but lie around and growl. Mail in.

May 11.—Heavy rifle fire all night. Was out from 8 a.m. till noon bossing up Royal Marines at trench-digging. Quiet morning, but heavy rifle and artillery fire in the afternoon. Yesterday, I was told, shrapnel pitched all round me in camp, tearing up the ground and smashing a rifle close to my head. I took no notice of it. I was asleep. Nice safe camps we have in these parts! The 29th Division (Irish) reported to be only two miles from our right flank today. Report confirmed later. Good news; something ought to be doing soon. Heavy naval firing going on in the distance. Heard that 4.7" naval guns had been placed in position on "Pope's Hill," to our left. Wish they could lay out the

Turkish guns—especially "Asiatic Annie"—that keep warming us up in our dugouts; we are getting tired of the beggars.

Heard that the *Lusitania* had been submarined near the Irish coast. Poor devils!—it's a one-eyed kind of death to be drowned like rats in a trap. I'd a dashed sight rather be shot any day. "Commandeered" a can of butter, some cheese, jam, and potatoes, so have lived high today. "Virtue rewarded"—the stuff just smiled at me as I was passing the commissariat. I couldn't resist its blandishments. Anyway, the quarter-master is always complaining about the "non-keeping" qualities of his provisions. And, when all's said and done, it's simply a raiding of the Philistines. How does the water get into our rum? Some rain today, cloudy, overcast skies, and not at all warm.

May 12.—Rum and not watered! Rained all night; place a quag-mire this morning. Got hold of some sacks and managed to sleep more or less dry. Have neither waterproof sheet nor blankets. Heard that all our blankets left behind on ship had been taken for wounded. If that is where they have gone we don't mind; sick men need them more than we do. Rather quiet night; expect both sides too wet and miserable to worry about killing each other. Didn't go out last night; thought I might as well stay in and nurse my shoulder, which is doing real good. First night in for longish spell.

Went out this morning and bossed up a lot of marines at trench-digging. It rained all the time and the ground was as sticky as fish-glue. Climbing up to "Quinn's Post" in this kind of weather is like the Johnnie in *Pilgrim's Progress* who found his swag growing bigger and heavier the farther he went. You can hardly lift your feet owing to the amount of Turkey sticking to them, and for every two yards you ad-vance you slide back more than one. And coming down is just as bad, although a deal speedier. You start off gingerly, sit down suddenly—*squelch!*—and when your wind comes back you find yourself at the foot of the hill with a sniper biffing away at you and enjoying the joke. It's quite funny—to read about.

My clothing is getting sadly in need of repair. Nothing to repair it with, however. Enemy's shells passing barely twenty feet above my dugout—a bit too close for comfort. Thinking of shifting my camp. Today the cap from one of our own shells passed clean through a man in a dugout just above my own, and injured another. Our gunners do things like that of a time: perhaps they imagine we need a little more excitement—or have a perverted sense of humour. Heavy distant fir-ing: the fleet at it again, I suppose.

May 13.—Came in at midnight after a spell of sapping—or, rather, watching others sap. Went on camp fatigue carrying water, fetching firewood for the cooks, etc. Can do this all right with one good arm. Otherwise had a light day. Australian Light Horse Brigade arrived from Egypt (minus horses), and now manning trenches as infantrymen. Employed my spare time in deepening my dug-out and fixing things up generally in my camp. Tremendous firing by ships last night; something doing. Fairly quiet day, with occasional bursts of rifle fire by both sides; also a little shelling. Noticed the following painted on some of our shells: "Turkish Delight: distributed free!" Went out at 8 p.m. to dig communication trench from "Shrapnel Gully" up to firing line on "Pope's Hill."

The position was a very exposed one, as we had to carry the trench up over a ridge open to enemy fire at fairly close range. It couldn't possibly have been done in daylight, so we were sent out to get a hustle on and complete the job before morning. Even as it was the Turks must have taken a tumble to our game, for they kept up a hot fire on the crest of the ridge all night long. As I couldn't use my arm I was put on sentry-go, and spent hour after hour lying in the scrub with the bullets hissing and spitting in the air round my head or knocking sparks out of the flinty soil. It wasn't a bit jolly.

We ran into a dead man while we were working—a Ceylon chap—who must have lain there since the landing. One of our chaps went down to camp and fetched up a *padre*—a fine old sort—who stood up and read the Burial Service under fire, and remained on the ridge until we had buried the corpse. I forget the parson's name, but I fancy he was the same man who worked at stretcher-bearing all through the first night in company with a Roman Catholic priest. There was a yarn going the rounds about this priest having taken part in a bayonet charge near "Quinn's": he denied it,—but well, from what I saw of him, I feel more than half inclined to believe it. We also found a dead Turkish officer. He had evidently been sketching round about these parts, his sketching wallet containing many drawings lying beside him. I wasn't lucky enough to get away with a specimen.

May 14.—Quiet morning for this locality. A little shelling plus some bombing. Enemy now taking to writing messages on pieces of paper, wrapping a stone in the paper and chucking the things into our trenches. They seem to imagine we have lost touch altogether with the world at large, and have taken it on themselves to furnish us with news. We are surprised to learn that fourteen British battleships have been sunk by the forts at the Narrows, that Egypt is in a state of revolt, and that the Germans are preparing to invade England, They asked us to treat our prisoners well, and they would do likewise with theirs. In a further message (an ultimatum) they called on us to surrender with our whole bag of tricks inside sixteen hours, and on receiving our reply—more forcible than elegant—some merry dog chucked back the following: "Well, if you won't surrender *we* will. Suppose we both surrender!"

Were served out with a new kind of biscuit today. It looks and tastes like stale bread, but when soaked in water and fried in fat it goes down well. I now save all the fat I can from my morning rasher of bacon, storing it in a jam-tin. I find it useful for cooking "chips" (when there happens to be any "spuds" about); also for greasing the bolt of my rifle. Speaking of bacon reminds me of a little picnic that happened a few nights ago. Two of us were passing the A.S.C. stores down in the "Gully." There was much store of jam, bacon, cheese, etc., piled in boxes on one side of the track. Now the back of this lordly stack of cases rested against a high but slender bank. In front was the camp of the attendant satellites. The thought seemed to strike us both at the same time. We acted on it right away. Putting in a short drive through the bank we struck oil—spelled, in this case, J-A-M. Since then I have done another little bit of prospecting round about that claim. I feel like having ham for breakfast; therefore I shall pay another visit to our drive, remove the bush that secures its entrance, and——!

Our stores are mostly brought up from the beach by mules, Indian drivers having charge of the stubborn animals. I am bound to say, however, these Indians seem able to do anything with their charges. They are very fond of them, too, and they (the mules) look fat and well cared for. I believe the drivers would almost as soon die as see such a fate overtake their beasts. Here is a case in point which I witnessed myself: a shell exploded bang above the track on which a transport team was making its way beachward. A mule staggered and came down on one knee, then righted itself. The driver examined the limb carefully, and finding the damage only amounted to the loss of a bit of skin, he threw his arms round the animal's neck and kissed it on the nose. I couldn't help wondering if he'd have kissed his wife in a like case.

Weather growing hotter daily. Flies increasing all the time. Flowers coming into bloom fast. Eased my feet by changing socks from left to right—the only change I could manage. Rockets thrown up by the

Turks last night. Wonder what the game is? Fancy homing pigeons are being used by the enemy, as I have noticed quite a lot flying about lately. *May* be wild ones, of course. Went on trenching same as yesterday.

May 15.—Heavy firing during night. New Zealanders stormed enemy's trenches to the left of our position last night and held them against strong counter attacks. Reported loss 500. A good bit of work well carried out. Antwerp and Ostend reported to be recaptured. Submarines said to be cruising off Anzac Cove, and all transports have left in consequence. H.M.S. *Lion* said to have been torpedoed; didn't know she was nearer than the North Sea. Went up to "Quinn's" at noon to go on sapping, etc. Some sniping, but little damage. Wish we could get the dead buried: the stench takes a lot of getting used to. Fairly quiet night.

Three weeks tomorrow since we landed! As lively a three weeks as any man could wish for. It seems like three months. But it's got to be done. And if I am lucky enough to get through this slather-up I mean to live a man of peace for the rest of my natural: get on to a tidy little place, grow spuds and cabbages, and raise early chickens—and kiddies!

CHAPTER 9

Sitting Tight

May 16.—Went on sapping, this time at "Pope's Hill." Had a man killed here in rather curious way. He was in the act of throwing out a shovelful of dirt when a bullet struck the blade of the shovel as it appeared for an instant above the parapet, came right down the handle, and knocked the poor chap's brains over his tunic. Rough luck! Came off work at noon. Quiet evening; some artillery and machine-gun fire. Another of our officers killed by a sniper today. A smart sort he was, too, and popular with all in the corps. Rum and tobacco issued— always an event. But why do they give us "medium strength" when nine out of ten of our chaps have been used to hard tack?

This soft stuff only burns our tongues and makes us say our prayers backwards. Got to bed early and was lulled to sleep by the music of bursting bombs and heavy rifle fire in the neighbourhood of "Quinn's" and "Courtney's." Our camp is at the foot of the cliff to the left of "Dead Man's Ridge," only thirty yards behind the firing line; all day and night we hear the song of bullets and the scream of shells passing overhead. I expect we'll miss them when we retire into private life again—if any of us are left to do the retiring stunt. One of our cooks shot dead while bending over his pots. Oh, it's a sweet spot, is Anzac!

Weather growing much warmer. Seems to agree with the flies. Wonder what part in the scheme of Nature flies play?

May 17.—Very heavy rifle and machine-gun fire in early part of night, followed by bombs galore. It seems that a company of Australian infantry stormed an enemy trench, but had to retire from it later on with considerable loss. Queer that such small bodies should be sent to attack a strong position. Did a five-hour spell of sapping at "Pope's." Snipers active, but were well protected, suffering no loss. Fairly quiet day. Some artillery fire. One of our naval guns got on to the enemy's trenches and blew them about in fine style with lyddite. Rumoured that Italy has come in on Allies' side. Also that Bulgaria has taken off the gloves, but on which side no one seems to know. My own opinion is that she'll side with Germany, simply because she *seems* so friendly towards the Allies.

I wouldn't trust one of those Balkan Staters farther than I could see him. Rumania will probably join the Allies—when it suits her. As for Greece, from what I saw of the Greeks in Lemnos and elsewhere, I reckon she doesn't count in the deal. Her men were born with deflated rubber tyres instead of backbones. Rumours fill the air. Stuck up the Q.M.S. for a shirt. He has promised to do his best. Hope I'll get one, as at present I don't possess such an article, and in this weather a knitted woollen cardigan impregnated with sweat and powdered clay isn't the most comfortable garment to wear next one's skin. Ordered to go on again on the old four-hour shifts at "Pope's," bossing up infantry at trench-digging. Would rather do a bigger spell right off the reel, as we get more sleep.

May 18.—Enemy throwing 10" or 12" shells (howitzers) right into the "Gully" among the thickly clustered dugouts. The explosions are fine to watch (so long as your own home doesn't suffer), dirt, stones, etc. being hurled 200 yards around. I don't think they killed very many, but the Light Horse chaps are fair mad at the way their camp has been knocked about. One fellow whose dugout had utterly vanished, its place being now occupied by a crater like a young volcano, wanted to know what the Government was thinking about.

Navy officers inspected our lines yesterday. Heard that they weren't much impressed with the work of our field batteries. This morning the troops were withdrawn from some of our trenches and the warships bombarded the Turks just in advance of our firing line, blowing trenches, sandbags, etc. up in fine style. The enemy kept pretty quiet afterwards; expect they were cleaning up things. Heard that the naval chaps are mounting 4.7" and 6" guns here; also that the Royal Artillery have arrived with two 12" howitzers. They are badly needed, as we don't seem able to silence the Turkish big guns.

Easy day on the whole. Still waiting for my shirt. Rumoured that the enemy has been strongly reinforced, and may try a big assault at any time. Also, that 20,000 well-armed Armenians have risen against the Turks. Also, that Italy has certainly joined in—not confirmed. Also, that Greece wants certain "guarantees" before coming in with the

Allies. Turkish losses since war started reported as 60 *per cent*. Hard to credit. More "Jack Johnsons" this afternoon. An enemy big gun discovered to be using a tunnel; when about to fire she is run out on rails, being run back into the tunnel the instant the shot is discharged. One up for the Turks! They are as 'cute as a cageful of monkeys.

May 19.—Enemy attacked in force last night. The rifle and machine-gun fire was something to write home about! The Turks came on in their usual close formation, and were simply mown down. They just melted away in places like a snowball in hell. Mostly they failed to reach our trenches, being cut down and beaten back by the terrific fire. In some cases, however, they did actually get into our front fire trenches, but were immediately bayoneted to a man. In other places they reached our parapets—only to be pulled by the legs *into* the trench by one man and bayoneted by another. It was a queer, mixed-up style of fighting, that suited our Australasian troops right down to the ground.

The attack was repulsed all along the line, finally dying away at about 2 a.m. Two hours later they had another try to push us over the ridge, advancing under cover of the heaviest artillery fire we have so far experienced. Again they attacked our whole line, finally concentrating on our right flank. At one point a New Zealand crowd left their trenches and charged the advancing Turks with the bayonet. They drove the enemy back in fine style, but suffered considerably themselves. Otherwise, however, the attack was repulsed with heavy loss to the enemy, our own casualties I hear being slight. I should think the Turks must be getting fed up with these attempts to drive us into the sea.

Heavy firing going on at all points as I write—rifles, Maxims, and artillery. The row is something awful! Enemy using shrapnel chiefly, and sweeping the "Gully" right down to the beach. Heard that the "Jack Johnsons" yesterday killed only about six men and wounded a few more. It seems almost incredible considering the way they pumped them into our camps. The soil here is mostly clayey and fairly free from rock, and the big shells, like our own lyddite, simply blow a huge hole, or crater, in the ground; and although the effect is rather fearsome the damage, unless close in, doesn't amount to much. If they pitched in rocky country I should say there would be a very different yarn to spin.

Heard that the *Lizzie* pitched a big shell slap into the tunnel in which a Turkish "Jack Johnson" was hiding and that she hasn't given tongue since. Also that the enemy tapped one of our field telephone wires *behind* our lines, and gave the General Staff twenty-four hours in which to clear us off the Peninsula, failing which he would blow us into the sea with big guns. Got my shirt at last, and feel a new man. If I could only raise a pair of trousers I'd be satisfied. I like plenty of fresh air and ventilation—but not in my nether garments.

Later.—A tremendous rifle and artillery fire took place this evening, continuing for an hour or so. Accounted for by New Zealand infantry attempting to capture some Turkish guns. They didn't go on with the venture, however, as the guns were too well guarded. Rather quiet evening afterwards. Been ordered to go on sapping at "Quinn's Post" tomorrow at 7 a.m.

Still Later.—Rather a funny thing happened tonight. We were ordered to rig up portable entanglements in front of our fire trenches at "Quinn's." Now as the enemy's trench and our own were separated by only a few yards it meant a quick death (and a verdict of "suicide while temporarily insane") to anyone attempting to even mount the parapet, much less starting in to a job of the kind out in the open. You should have seen the chaps' faces (and heard their prayers) when the order came along. Of course they all realised it was a mistake, the order being cancelled later on. The entanglements were there, however, so our officer thought it would be a bright idea to shove them out in front by means of long spars. After a lot of trouble we managed this, and they looked real good standing heads and tails along the front of our trenches. But when the Turks threw out light grapnels attached to ropes and dragged the things back to do duty for *them,* they didn't look half so good. And the infantry laughed some. We went to bed.

May 20.—Quiet morning. No enemy artillery fire and only a little of our own. Later some shelling by both sides. Worked at erecting overhead cover on the support trenches at "Quinn's"—originally the fire trenches, the outcome of the line of holes dug after the landing. Funny kind of job: every time you showed a hand above the parapet the Turks had a shot at it. From 6.30 till about 7.30 all firing ceased on both sides. It was the first time we had experienced absolute quiet since our arrival here, and the sensation was a strange one. It was still stranger to hear the song of the lark; I reckon the birds sized it up as the end of the Great War, for they seemed to all slip out of their dugouts at once. Heard it was a truce to allow the Turks to bring in their wounded. When the firing began again it was something to listen to!

80

Big guns and little guns, they all seemed to be working overtime. They kept it up most of the night, too.

May 21.—On overhead cover same as yesterday. Fairly quiet all round. More rumours! Another truce talked of. Heard that quite a lot of prisoners surrendered today. Orders sent round that everything possible was to be done to encourage enemy to desert. Which reminds me——

A few nights ago three Turks were captured by a patrol and brought into camp. They said in broken English that they'd been trying to surrender. They were taken down to headquarters to be questioned, and later on sent back to our camp, the O.C. receiving orders to feed them up well, then give the beggars a chance to escape. The idea was that they would return to their own lines, tell their chums of the fine time they'd had in our camp, and thus cause a lot of deserting from the enemy. Nothing of this was to be said to them, of course.

Well, we took our prisoners down to the cook's quarters and gave them the time of their lives. They ate about a tin of jam each, *ditto* of condensed milk, showed a marked appreciation for the army biscuits, and (they couldn't have been true believers—or else they were just as much in the dark as ourselves regarding the contents) tackled the bully beef with gusto, finishing up with Woodbine cigarettes. They weren't game to sample the rum, however, but it wasn't wasted. When they were full up to the back teeth we asked them if they knew where there was any firewood to be got, as most of the big stuff had been cut out of the "Gully." Yes, they did know of some, but to get it they would have to crawl up close to their own lines.

Things couldn't be better, we thought; they were told to clear out and get some. Away they went, up a deep *nullah* that bisected our lines—and returned a couple of hours later loaded up with brushwood like walking Christmas Trees! At their own request we led them back to the cookhouse, saw them started on a fresh supply of jam and condensed milk, and gave the thing up as a bad job. Catch them letting their mates into the secret of all those good things! Indeed, most of our prisoners were only too pleased to remain with us once we'd caught them. We set them to various jobs, and, to do them justice, they worked away quite cheerfully, never, so far as I know, attempting to escape from a place where they were so well fed and got free smokes. The Australians installed one as camp barber, and the blue-jackets from the fleet used to grin at the spectacle of a big husky Turk going round his enemy's throat with a keen-edged razor.

About this time most of us had grown full beards. I don't know who originated the style, but it got to be the fashion to trim our beards to a point *à la* His Majesty. Then our slouch hats underwent the trimming process, the result being a far-fetched jockey's cap. Then nearly every chap cut his slacks or breeches off well above the knee, and a great many discarded *puttees*. Others shore their shirt-sleeves off shoulder high. Still others went without their shirts altogether in the daytime, going naked from the waist up. So you can guess what the Anzac Army looked like! No wonder the Turks did a bolt when our ragtime mob of toughs rushed them with the bayonet! They looked like a crowd of sundowners who had struck an outback trail and got badly bushed in a dry season.

May 22.—Went up to "Quinn's" at 7 a.m. to go on with sticking up overhead cover. Rather rainy morning. Mud—and such mud!- everywhere. Work of art climbing hill owing to feet caking inches deep with the sticky clay soil. Just got started to work when taken off to make loopholes in a new front fire trench—enemy's trench being only about fifteen yards away. Trench badly exposed to cross-fire from machine-guns well placed on rising ground. All around were splashes of blood. Australian officer informed us that a number of his men had been shot while lying at the *bottom* of this trench. Did what we could, but as fast as we stuck the sandbags up they were cut to pieces and blown down by Maxim fire. Bombed out many times. Had many narrow shaves. Forced to give it best and wait till dark, when we'll have another try. All these dirty jobs seem to fall to the engineers.

Rain cleared off in afternoon. Mail came in today. Got four letters—very satisfactory. "Jack Johnsons" at work again. Snipers also busy; bagged quite a lot of our chaps today. *Our* snipers are beginning to thin them down, however. Our trench mortars emptied bombs finely into enemy's trenches lately. Fairly quiet night, with rifle fire going oif in bursts now and then.

May 23.—Went on at "Quinn" again, loopholing and strengthening fire trenches. Curious state of affairs here: *we* sapped out towards enemy's lines some time ago—and met the Turks doing the same towards us. Result: *a communicating trench from our lines into his*, which is guarded night and day at either end by each party respectively, the intervening distance being about ten yards! Didn't dare to expose ourselves, as sharpshooters were sniping all the time from two sides, a cross-fire at a range of about forty yards. Got back to camp and found issue of rum awaiting me, also ration of *fresh* beef. Cooked it on a grill made of twisted fencing wire and had an A1 blow-out. More letters today. Wonder what the navy is doing at the Dardanelles? Rumours; the air is full of them. Here are three: (a) Turkey has demanded either £40,000,000 or £50,000,000 from Germany, otherwise she will join the Allies; (b) we are going to be relieved and sent home to England on the 25th instant, to refit; (c) submarines are cruising about quite close.

Today the warships bombarded the enemy's trenches just in front of our own, first giving us warning to keep our heads well down. Didn't need the warning, as shells simply skimmed our parapets. One plumped *into* a trench full of Australians. Didn't do much damage luckily, but upset the harmony of a nice little card-party playing poker. Result: the loss of some money and several tempers. Got a blanket served out today. Could have done with it a long time ago. Still waiting for trousers; the pair I own now on their last legs.

Talking of legs, I bumped into one today sticking out into one of our support trenches. You had to duck to pass it. Seems that our chaps when building the cover found a dead Turk badly in their way, and as they would have had some difficulty in removing him they decided to build him up *in* the roof; his leg slipped through, however, so they just let it hang. Quiet night; hardly any firing at any part of the line.

May 24.—Just finishing breakfast when rain started. The worst of it is that even a slight fall turns this country into a kind of clay bog, owing to the top soil clogging on one's boots and then slipping over the subsoil. It is like climbing a greased egg to scale the hills—and our position here is on top of a high ridge running round a deep gully. Coming down one generally does a joy slide on one's hindquarters. Have been ordered to stand by, pending a rumoured armistice supposed to take place at 7.30 a.m. Heard that Italy has come in on Allies' side: this time it seems to be credited. Hope it is true.

Later.—Armistice did take place, lasting till 4.30 p.m., for the purpose of burying the dead—or "planting stiffs," to give the occupation its local name. It was about time this was done. I never saw so many bodies crowded into the same space before; there were literally thousands of them. And the condition they were in! I dare not describe the sights I saw. We scraped out shallow holes, edged the things gingerly in and covered them up as quickly as possible. It paid to smoke hard all the time. I picked up a German officer's sword (broken off at the hilt), a Turkish *ditto*, and dozens of other war curios. I noticed a magnificent diamond ring on a Turkish officer's finger, but he was in such a state of putrefaction that I allowed him to retain it.

One cannot be too careful when working with decomposed bodies; if a cut finger happens to get into contact with putrid human flesh you'll know all about it. We mixed together, the enemy "undertakers" and our own. Some of the Turkish officers handed us cigarettes and spoke in fluent English. They were a fine, jolly-looking lot of fellows dressed in swagger uniforms. The Germans, however, stood at a distance and scowled. Our fellows returned their scowls with interest. They also favoured them with a salute (understood of all men) in which the thumb and fingers of one hand act in conjunction with the nose. The Huns didn't seem to appreciate the honour. A quiet night followed.

May 25.—Working at same job as before—loopholing trenches and generally strengthening position at "Quinn's Post." It wouldn't be difficult to get laid out at this game, for there is an almost continuous cross-fire playing a few inches above your head, and as fast as you stick up sandbags the machine-guns cut them into shreds.

Saw the *Triumph* torpedoed. She had been acting the part of dry nurse to our crowd off Anzac Cove, and it was like a death in the family when she went to the bottom. I was sitting in my dugout at the time it happened, eating the midday meal, and had a first-class view of the whole thing at a distance of about two and a half miles. From the height of our camp above sea-level we could even see the submarine, like a shadowy fish, below the water. She was reported to have been struck by two torpedoes; I saw only one, however—or its wake, rather. The projectile seemed to hit the warship right amidships, going through her nets as if they were made of paper. A tremendous cloud of dense brown smoke mixed with steam sprang aloft like a geyser, and the big ship listed over at once in the direction from which the torpedo had come.

At the same time she seemed to settle down in the water with a jump. The submarine couldn't have been more than 200 yards away when she launched the torpedo, which appeared to cut the water at a great bat. A destroyer was cruising about close handy, and she at once backed in against the battleship, the crew jumping and tumbling on board like rats. Meantime she (the destroyer) opened fire every time the submarine shoved her periscope above the surface. One shot was fired at a distance of only about fifty yards. The sea was soon alive with all kinds of small craft hastening to the work of rescue. In ten minutes the *Triumph* turned completely over, showing her bottom for all the world like a big whale, finally disappearing in about twenty minutes from the time of the explosion. She didn't dive—just slowly subsided. Many of the crew jumped overboard; through glasses we could see them struggling in the water.

Almost immediately a whole flotilla of torpedo boats and destroyers seemed to spring from nowhere, and started to hunt down the submarine. As I write they are steaming round and round in a big circle, an aeroplane hovering overhead and evidently directing operations; at the same time the enemy is pumping shrapnel into the bay from long range for all he is worth, evidently in the hope of bagging those engaged in the work of rescue. I have since seen it stated in the papers that the enemy's artillery was directed against the destroyers, and that the drowning men and those assisting them had to take their chance. Then why in the name of common sense did he use shrapnel? The contention is absurd. The Turks on the whole were clean fighters, but when the poor old *Triumph* went down they put a dirty blot on their record. I hope never to see another ship torpedoed; it was one of the saddest sights I ever witnessed.

Later.—Reported that the submarine was bagged after a long chase. Heavy rain this afternoon, and the whole place a bog. Hot sun afterwards which turned the bog into a glue deposit. Things fairly quiet, as they have been for the last two or three days. Enemy doesn't seem to like our bombs thrown from trench mortars. They are a Japanese invention, and when they pitch into the Turkish trenches they fairly raise hell—and human remains! Heard that over 400 were lost in the *Triumph*: hope it isn't true. Finding enemy was mining towards our trenches we put in a counter mine. Enemy exploded his—and ours at the same time. *W-o-o-o-o-uf!* she went. So did the writer—bringing up waist deep in a heap of soft sticky clay, hard jam tins, and discarded accoutrements at the foot of the ridge. Felt a bit "rocky" after being dug out. Left ear gone. Head queer. Hope it will come all right again. Had another issue of fresh beef this evening, the second, I fancy, since we landed. Cooked it on my own home-made grill and found it *kapai*. More rain.

Still Later.—Heard that losses on *Triumph* were very slight: about twenty or thirty. Rain cleared off and ground now drying fast. Fairly quiet night, except for some bombing. You get queer things in bombs sometimes, especially Turkish bombs. For instance: I was working in one of the advanced saps. There was a good deal of bombing going on a bit to my right. In the traverse next to where I was sapping a captured Turkish gramophone was being made to work overtime in *The Turkish Patrol*, for the edification of an Australian audience. Presently—*Bang!* It was a bomb, thrown slap into the concert party. The music ceased. Followed the customary volley of blasphemy in back-blocks Australian. Then, to my surprise, a roar of laughter echoed round the traverse. Naturally I waltzed along to see what had happened—and found a very profane Australian seated in the bottom of the trench nursing his wounds. He looked for all the world as if he had been scrapping with a whole colony of porcupines, and was bleeding from a score or two of wounds.

"It's needles from the bomb," laughed one of his mates, in answer to my astonished look. "The poor devil's that full up of gramophone needles, if we only had a *something* record we could play a *something* tune on him!"

But we weren't a bit slow at faking up bombs ourselves. I have known rusty nails, bits of shells, flints, cartridge cases, fragments of broken periscopes—anything, in fact, that came along shoved into a home-made jam-tin bomb. Once some of the chaps heaved over a 7-lb. jam-can filled with ham and bacon bones. You ought to have heard the jamboree in the Turkish trench when the unclean animal's mortal remains blew round their ears! They didn't half like being shot by pig. On another occasion some Australians informed me that they wanted "a hell of a knock-out bomb," as they had located a Turkish listening post close up to our front line trenches.

I manufactured one of the "hair-brush" variety, using *two 15-oz. slabs of guncotton*, and packing round the explosive about three pounds of assorted projectiles; the whole thing I wrapped up in a whole sandbag and wound it round and round with barbed wire. When completed it looked a pretty little toy about the size of a respectable ham. I own I had some misgivings about being able to throw it the required length. However, the distance was only a matter of a few yards, and I got it fair into the desired spot. When she went off bang there wasn't much of that listening post left, while as for the Turks who manned it—well, I guess they're going still!

"Quinn's Post" was always a rotten shop for bombs. At first the Turks had things pretty much their own way in that line. Time after time they cleared our front trenches by bomb-throwing, and then rushed the position; and I can tell you it called for some hard hand-to-hand fighting on our part to get them out again. But we always did it; good soldiers as they are they couldn't live in the same township with our chaps when cold steel was the order of the day. There isn't much fun left in life once you've had eighteen inches of rusty bayonet shoved through your gizzard. The Turks don't fear death; if killed in action they believe they go straight to Paradise and have a high old time with the girls. But you can't blame a man if he wished to have a little more practice on earth—nor for being a bit particular about the manner in which he started on the long trail. I reckon that's how it was with them. I don't blame them, either; it's a sloppy kind of death, the bayonet one.

After a time we got top-dog in the bombing line. Our system was a simple one: for every bomb the enemy threw into us we gave him at least *two* in return. He didn't like it a little bit. At first we used to throw the bombs back again as fast as they came in, the fuses being timed a bit too long; afterwards, however, that game didn't pay, quite a lot of poor chaps getting laid out through the things exploding in their hands. Dropping a sandbag or an overcoat on them took most of the sting out of the beggars, and it wasn't long till every third man's great-coat looked as if it had been in a railway accident—or a cyclone.

One night I shan't forget in a hurry. It simply rained bombs. Man after man went down. The trench was a shambles. On came the Turks, carrying our fire trench with ease; there was really nothing to stop them. They got right into our support trench. Then our chaps got to work. We bombed them back. They came again. Again we cleared them out. The position was carried and recarried four separate times, eventually remaining in our hands. Reader, I wish you had seen those trenches when the picnic was finished. It took us a long time cleaning them up. There were all kinds of queer things sticking to the sides and to the overhead cover. One of our chaps put the thing in a nutshell. "I don't give a *something* what the *padre* says," he observed, "there'll be an all-fired mix-up when they go aloft! "

"Quinn's" was in truth the limit. I reckon you could get killed there a dashed sight easier than anywhere in the whole line. It was just fair hell with all the doors open. It was the place where V.C.'s were earned—but not given! Come to think of it, it would have taken a sackful to go round. Yes, that must have been the reason.

CHAPTER 10

The Order of the Push

Several Months Later.—I have just been discharged from my second English hospital, and am at present on "leave pending discharge from the Service, '*Permanently Unfit.*'" I feel pretty well that way, too. My soldiering days are over: henceforth I am a man of peace. Well, I've had a goodish innings and can't complain, even in spite of the fact that I'll never be quite the same man again. And, after all, things might be a deal worse: I might be one of those grotesque-looking bundles of khaki and rat-picked bones now lying unburied and forgotten in the scrub of Gaba Tepe, for instance. And I'd go through it all again—aye, a hundred times sooner than have the women call me "slacker"! I say "*women*" advisedly: the "*men*" are all wearing khaki now; those "*she*-men" who aren't don't count—*they* are just white-livered, cold-footed, rubber-spined swine! That's straight Anzac.

I'd cheerfully forfeit a month's back pay to watch one of the slacker brigade read these lines, and to know that away down in the little dried-up kernel he calls his heart there still exists enough red blood to pump a flush of shame into his white girl's cheeks. "Girl," did I say? Then I ask the "gentler" sex to forgive me, for well I know that nine out of every ten women in the British Empire have far more true pluck and sand in their little fingers than the whole slacker brigade have in their useless tender-footed bodies. What right have these damned cowards to go to theatres, dances, football matches, and concerts; to lie warm in bed at night and eat soft tucker by day—to live their soft, easy-going useless lives, while I and the like of me have to go out and live, fight—aye, and die—like beasts?

True, we volunteered; we just had to—being *men*! What right (I put it straight to any slacker whose eye now rests on this page—if he hasn't already chucked this little volume into the fire)—what right have you, you little white-livered cur, you slimy maggot—what right have you to wear the dress and ape the bearing of a *man*? What will you say to the *men* when they return from doing their bit—when they ask why *you* didn't roll up and help them in their need? That you were a conscientious objector? That you didn't believe in shedding human blood? That you had to stay at home—and make money—while *they* were fighting and sweating that the old home might not be polluted by the shadow of the German beasts, the ravishers of poor little Belgium? Well, you can say what you like. But I know what they will call you—a name that no man worth calling a man ever takes unchallenged from his fellows—what I call you right now: COWARD!

I was going to add: What will you say to your children when they ask you what *you* did in The Great War? But surely no woman will ever call you husband and bear your children! If such women are to be found, and I only had the power, I'd emasculate you all rather than see your dirty breed perpetuated.

That's some more straight Australasian. But to come back to the matter in hand, as the public tub-thumpers say——

I got in the way of some bullets. I didn't want to, but they were flying round pretty lively and I bagged a few—one through the arm, another through the shoulder (it's still sticking somewhere down under the blade), two pieces of explosive bullet in my right hand (still there and letting me know it when I write), plus an assortment of small splinters distributed round about my figure-head. My left ear is gone; I don't sleep too well; there is a fitter's shop doing great work day and night in my head, and when I walk out to take the air things are apt to spin round some, and I fancy the dear old ladies imagine I suffer from chronic alcoholism. Altogether I don't feel quiet as good as I did before I went on tour with the Anzacs.

Neither did the medical board, so they're giving me the tinware. Funny thing: my appetite is quite good, and I look as strong as a horse. Hence the aforesaid old ladies are always telling how well I look, and hoping I am *quite* recovered from my wounds. At first this sort of thing used to bore me; now, however, it only amuses me. It's a boncer gift is the saving grace of humour, and keeps a fellow from getting into the blues when he compares the man he was once with the man he is now. However, that's by the way.

I have been in six hospitals altogether. I don't want any more, not being greedy. I am fed up with hospitals, fed up with doctors, fed up with nurses ("sisters" we called them), and, above all, fed up and surfeited with the old blue suit! Not that we weren't well treated in hospital. I have nothing much to complain of (although they did in some cases treat us like kids): I have much to praise. The doctors were on the whole a decent crowd; the sisters were just angels! I take my hat off to them wishing them a long and jolly life on this old planet and a featherbed in Heaven when they hit the long trail. *Kia Ora!*

After being hit I was taken in a fleet sweeper to Lemnos Island, about forty-five miles from Anzac. I was in two hospitals there. From Lemnos Island I went in a hospital ship to Alexandria, and on by hospital train to Cairo. I put in a spell there, and was then shipped (by train!) to Port Said. From Port Said I was consigned to England, where I brought up in Cardiff. Finally I did a spell in a South Coast hospital. Then they got sick of me. The feeling was mutual. So I'm getting the order of the push.

Taking it all in all I've had a kind of a Cook's Personally Conducted Tour. I've had good times and bad times, the good fairly well balancing the bad. On the whole it has been a most interesting trip. It has also been to a certain extent an exciting trip. I reckon it's up to me to remember the good times and forget the bad. And I wouldn't have missed it, good or bad, for worlds.

For, dear reader (please don't think I'm bragging), I'd rather be lying this moment in an unknown grave in the Gallipoli Peninsula than be branded for life as a God damned slacker!

That isn't swearing. It's a pious expression. And, take it either way, it's pardonable.

LEONAUR

ALSO FROM LEONAUR
AVAILABLE IN SOFTCOVER OR HARDCOVER WITH DUST JACKET

ADVENTURES OF A YOUNG RIFLEMAN *by Johann Christian Maempel*—The Experiences of a Saxon in the French & British Armies During the Napoleonic Wars.

THE HUSSAR *by Norbert Landsheit & G. R. Gleig*—A German Cavalryman in British Service Throughout the Napoleonic Wars.

RECOLLECTIONS OF THE PENINSULA *by Moyle Sherer*—An Officer of the 34th Regiment of Foot—'The Cumberland Gentlemen'—on Campaign Against Napoleon's French Army in Spain.

MARINE OF REVOLUTION & CONSULATE *by Moreau de Jonnès*—The Recollections of a French Soldier of the Revolutionary Wars 1791-1804.

GENTLEMEN IN RED *by John Dobbs & Robert Knowles*—Two Accounts of British Infantry Officers During the Peninsular War Recollections of an Old 52nd Man by John Dobbs An Officer of Fusiliers by Robert Knowles.

CORPORAL BROWN'S CAMPAIGNS IN THE LOW COUNTRIES *by Robert Brown*—Recollections of a Coldstream Guard in the Early Campaigns Against Revolutionary France 1793-1795.

THE 7TH (QUEENS OWN) HUSSARS: Volume 2—1793-1815 *by C. R. B. Barrett*—During the Campaigns in the Low Countries & the Peninsula and Waterloo Campaigns of the Napoleonic Wars. Volume 2: 1793-1815.

THE MARENGO CAMPAIGN 1800 *by Herbert H. Sargent*—The Victory that Completed the Austrian Defeat in Italy.

DONALDSON OF THE 94TH—SCOTS BRIGADE *by Joseph Donaldson*—The Recollections of a Soldier During the Peninsula & South of France Campaigns of the Napoleonic Wars.

A CONSCRIPT FOR EMPIRE *by Philippe as told to Johann Christian Maempel*—The Experiences of a Young German Conscript During the Napoleonic Wars.

JOURNAL OF THE CAMPAIGN OF 1815 *by Alexander Cavalié Mercer*—The Experiences of an Officer of the Royal Horse Artillery During the Waterloo Campaign.

NAPOLEON'S CAMPAIGNS IN POLAND 1806-7 *by Robert Wilson*—The campaign in Poland from the Russian side of the conflict.

LEONAUR

ALSO FROM LEONAUR

AVAILABLE IN SOFTCOVER OR HARDCOVER WITH DUST JACKET

OMPTEDA OF THE KING'S GERMAN LEGION *by Christian von Ompteda*—A Hanoverian Officer on Campaign Against Napoleon.

LIEUTENANT SIMMONS OF THE 95TH (RIFLES) *by George Simmons*—Recollections of the Peninsula, South of France & Waterloo Campaigns of the Napoleonic Wars.

A HORSEMAN FOR THE EMPEROR *by Jean Baptiste Gazzola*—A Cavalryman of Napoleon's Army on Campaign Throughout the Napoleonic Wars.

SERGEANT LAWRENCE *by William Lawrence*—With the 40th Regt. of Foot in South America, the Peninsular War & at Waterloo.

CAMPAIGNS WITH THE FIELD TRAIN *by Richard D. Henegan*—Experiences of a British Officer During the Peninsula and Waterloo Campaigns of the Napoleonic Wars.

CAVALRY SURGEON *by S. D. Broughton*—On Campaign Against Napoleon in the Peninsula & South of France During the Napoleonic Wars 1812-1814.

MEN OF THE RIFLES *by Thomas Knight, Henry Curling & Jonathan Leach*—The Reminiscences of Thomas Knight of the 95th (Rifles) by Thomas Knight, Henry Curling's Anecdotes by Henry Curling & The Field Services of the Rifle Brigade from its Formation to Waterloo by Jonathan Leach.

THE ULM CAMPAIGN 1805 *by F. N. Maude*—Napoleon and the Defeat of the Austrian Army During the 'War of the Third Coalition'.

SOLDIERING WITH THE 'DIVISION' *by Thomas Garrety*—The Military Experiences of an Infantryman of the 43rd Regiment During the Napoleonic Wars.

SERGEANT MORRIS OF THE 73RD FOOT *by Thomas Morris*—The Experiences of a British Infantryman During the Napoleonic Wars-Including Campaigns in Germany and at Waterloo.

A VOICE FROM WATERLOO *by Edward Cotton*—The Personal Experiences of a British Cavalryman Who Became a Battlefield Guide and Authority on the Campaign of 1815.

NAPOLEON AND HIS MARSHALS *by J. T. Headley*—The Men of the First Empire.

LEONAUR

ALSO FROM LEONAUR
AVAILABLE IN SOFTCOVER OR HARDCOVER WITH DUST JACKET

BUGEAUD: A PACK WITH A BATON *by Thomas Robert Bugeaud*—The Early Campaigns of a Soldier of Napoleon's Army Who Would Become a Marshal of France.

WATERLOO RECOLLECTIONS *by Frederick Llewellyn*—Rare First Hand Accounts, Letters, Reports and Retellings from the Campaign of 1815.

SERGEANT NICOL *by Daniel Nicol*—The Experiences of a Gordon Highlander During the Napoleonic Wars in Egypt, the Peninsula and France.

THE JENA CAMPAIGN: 1806 *by F. N. Maude*—The Twin Battles of Jena & Auerstadt Between Napoleon's French and the Prussian Army.

PRIVATE O'NEIL *by Charles O'Neil*—The recollections of an Irish Rogue of H. M. 28th Regt.—The Slashers—during the Peninsula & Waterloo campaigns of the Napoleonic war.

ROYAL HIGHLANDER *by James Anton*—A soldier of H.M 42nd (Royal) Highlanders during the Peninsular, South of France & Waterloo Campaigns of the Napoleonic Wars.

CAPTAIN BLAZE *by Elzéar Blaze*—Life in Napoleons Army.

LEJEUNE VOLUME 1 *by Louis-François Lejeune*—The Napoleonic Wars through the Experiences of an Officer on Berthier's Staff.

LEJEUNE VOLUME 2 *by Louis-François Lejeune*—The Napoleonic Wars through the Experiences of an Officer on Berthier's Staff.

CAPTAIN COIGNET *by Jean-Roch Coignet*—A Soldier of Napoleon's Imperial Guard from the Italian Campaign to Russia and Waterloo.

FUSILIER COOPER *by John S. Cooper*—Experiences in the 7th (Royal) Fusiliers During the Peninsular Campaign of the Napoleonic Wars and the American Campaign to New Orleans.

FIGHTING NAPOLEON'S EMPIRE *by Joseph Anderson*—The Campaigns of a British Infantryman in Italy, Egypt, the Peninsular & the West Indies During the Napoleonic Wars.

CHASSEUR BARRES *by Jean-Baptiste Barres*—The experiences of a French Infantryman of the Imperial Guard at Austerlitz, Jena, Eylau, Friedland, in the Peninsular, Lutzen, Bautzen, Zinnwald and Hanau during the Napoleonic Wars.

LEONAUR

ALSO FROM LEONAUR
AVAILABLE IN SOFTCOVER OR HARDCOVER WITH DUST JACKET

LIFE IN THE ARMY OF NORTHERN VIRGINIA by Carlton McCarthy— The Observations of a Confederate Artilleryman of Cutshaw's Battalion During the American Civil War 1861-1865.

HISTORY OF THE CAVALRY OF THE ARMY OF THE POTOMAC by Charles D. Rhodes—Including Pope's Army of Virginia and the Cavalry Operations in West Virginia During the American Civil War.

CAMP-FIRE AND COTTON-FIELD by Thomas W. Knox—A New York Herald Correspondent's View of the American Civil War.

SERGEANT STILLWELL by Leander Stillwell —The Experiences of a Union Army Soldier of the 61st Illinois Infantry During the American Civil War.

STONEWALL'S CANNONEER by Edward A. Moore—Experiences with the Rockbridge Artillery, Confederate Army of Northern Virginia, During the American Civil War.

THE SIXTH CORPS by George Stevens—The Army of the Potomac, Union Army, During the American Civil War.

THE RAILROAD RAIDERS by William Pittenger—An Ohio Volunteers Recollections of the Andrews Raid to Disrupt the Confederate Railroad in Georgia During the American Civil War.

CITIZEN SOLDIER by John Beatty—An Account of the American Civil War by a Union Infantry Officer of Ohio Volunteers Who Became a Brigadier General.

COX: PERSONAL RECOLLECTIONS OF THE CIVIL WAR--VOLUME 1 by Jacob Dolson Cox—West Virginia, Kanawha Valley, Gauley Bridge, Cotton Mountain, South Mountain, Antietam, the Morgan Raid & the East Tennessee Campaign.

COX: PERSONAL RECOLLECTIONS OF THE CIVIL WAR--VOLUME 2 by Jacob Dolson Cox—Siege of Knoxville, East Tennessee, Atlanta Campaign, the Nashville Campaign & the North Carolina Campaign.

KERSHAW'S BRIGADE VOLUME 1 by D. Augustus Dickert—Manassas, Seven Pines, Sharpsburg (Antietam), Fredricksburg, Chancellorsville, Gettysburg, Chickamauga, Chattanooga, Fort Sanders & Bean Station.

KERSHAW'S BRIGADE VOLUME 2 by D. Augustus Dickert—At the wilderness, Cold Harbour, Petersburg, The Shenandoah Valley and Cedar Creek..

LEONAUR

ALSO FROM LEONAUR
AVAILABLE IN SOFTCOVER OR HARDCOVER WITH DUST JACKET

ESCAPE FROM THE FRENCH *by Edward Boys*—A Young Royal Navy Midshipman's Adventures During the Napoleonic War.

THE VOYAGE OF H.M.S. PANDORA *by Edward Edwards R. N. & George Hamilton, edited by Basil Thomson*—In Pursuit of the Mutineers of the Bounty in the South Seas—1790-1791.

MEDUSA *by J. B. Henry Savigny and Alexander Correard and Charlotte-Adélaïde Dard* —Narrative of a Voyage to Senegal in 1816 & The Sufferings of the Picard Family After the Shipwreck of the Medusa.

THE SEA WAR OF 1812 VOLUME 1 *by A. T. Mahan*—A History of the Maritime Conflict.

THE SEA WAR OF 1812 VOLUME 2 *by A. T. Mahan*—A History of the Maritime Conflict.

WETHERELL OF H. M. S. HUSSAR *by John Wetherell*—The Recollections of an Ordinary Seaman of the Royal Navy During the Napoleonic Wars.

THE NAVAL BRIGADE IN NATAL *by C. R. N. Burne*—With the Guns of H. M. S. Terrible & H. M. S. Tartar during the Boer War 1899-1900.

THE VOYAGE OF H. M. S. BOUNTY *by William Bligh*—The True Story of an 18th Century Voyage of Exploration and Mutiny.

SHIPWRECK! *by William Gilly*—The Royal Navy's Disasters at Sea 1793-1849.

KING'S CUTTERS AND SMUGGLERS: 1700-1855 *by E. Keble Chatterton*—A unique period of maritime history-from the beginning of the eighteenth to the middle of the nineteenth century when British seamen risked all to smuggle valuable goods from wool to tea and spirits from and to the Continent.

CONFEDERATE BLOCKADE RUNNER *by John Wilkinson*—The Personal Recollections of an Officer of the Confederate Navy.

NAVAL BATTLES OF THE NAPOLEONIC WARS *by W. H. Fitchett*—Cape St. Vincent, the Nile, Cadiz, Copenhagen, Trafalgar & Others.

PRISONERS OF THE RED DESERT *by R. S. Gwatkin-Williams*—The Adventures of the Crew of the Tara During the First World War.

U-BOAT WAR 1914-1918 *by James B. Connolly/Karl von Schenk*—Two Contrasting Accounts from Both Sides of the Conflict at Sea D uring the Great War.

www.ingramcontent.com/pod-product-compliance
Lightning Source LLC
Chambersburg PA
CBHW032018090426
42741CB00006B/645